The LORD of PARABLES

LeRoy Lawson

STANDARD PUBLISHING
Cincinnati, Ohio
39981

Unless otherwise noted, all Scripture quotations are from the Holy Bible, New International Version, © 1978 by the New York International Bible Society. Used by permission of Zondervan Bible Publishers.

Sharing the thoughts of his own heart, the author may express views that are not entirely consistent with those of the publisher.

Library of Congress Cataloging in Publication Data:

Lawson, E. LeRoy, 1938-
  The Lord of parables.

    1. Jesus Christ—Parables.   2. Christian life—
1960-   .   I. Title.
BT335.2.L38   1984   226'.806   83-12640
ISBN 0-87239-707-6
ISBN 0-87239-706-8 (guide)

TABLE OF CONTENTS

INTRODUCTION

"Aren't you the same fellow who wrote that other study book on the parables?"

Yes, I'm the same fellow who wrote *Cracking the Code*, but these aren't the same parables, at least not all of them. For that matter, I'm not exactly the same writer, either.

Jesus' parables meet the reader where he is. Each reading yields different insights. They are so rich, so multifaceted in meaning, and so penetrating in personal application that they never lose their grip on you. As you grow older, they grow wiser. When you were a child, they were good stories; now that you are no longer a child, they are more than stories: they are wisdom itself, told by the wisest of them all.

They remind me of Arizona. To the untutored eye, this amazing state seems like nothing but arid wasteland. I'm not talking about the lush mountain areas to the north, of course, but the central desert. When we moved here, we wondered whether these children of the green Northwest could ever adjust to mountains without trees, rivers without water, and lawns without grass. Everywhere we looked we saw barrenness. One quick scanning of the horizon told all, we thought.

How wrong we were. After just a few years, we have learned to *see* what we are looking at. Now we marvel at the brilliant play of light and shadow as the sun moves across an ever-changing sky; we admire the bright, multi-colored waxen blossoms on the numerous types of cacti. We stoop to pick delicate ground flowers struggling against the desert heat, and pause to celebrate the heroic thrust of century plants silhouetted against the deepening sunset. We have become Arizonans, more mature now, enough so to respond to the incredible beauty of this enigmatic but seductive region.

Mature. Jesus' parables, simple enough a child can follow the story line, are as deceptively fertile to the mature reader as the Arizona desert has become to natives of the Oregon rain forests. They can still be read quickly, but when pondered, they yield a harvest of wisdom. This older writer, you see, is not exactly the same person who wrote *Cracking the Code*.

Several of the Scriptures this book studies could be cataloged as Jesus' "darker parables," comparable to the tragedies from Shakespeare's "dark period." Their themes are death and judgment and injustice on earth. They are not tales told by a youngster. They reflect ripe thought. The middle-aged reader, aware that his time is running out even as his mistakes and failures are compounding the case against him, listens intently as Jesus speaks of this world's end—and *his* end.

He identifies with the merciless laborers in the vineyard; this is how *he* has handled God. He is suffering his own "dark period" and needs the light of hope that Jesus offers. If a prodigal son can be saved, then there is hope for him. If the kingdom of God is like a banquet to which even the poor and lame are invited, maybe God wants him at His banquet table as well. If the laborer who worked only one hour can be recompensed as generously as the worker who put in a full day, maybe it is not too late for God to use him now.

So don't be turned off by "yet another study of the parables." Even though you may have thoroughly analyzed them before, you'll profit from another look. You, too, are older than when you last studied them. Renew your acquaintance with these stories that will never die. You'll be surprised how much they have learned in the past few years.

I should warn you, by the way, that these are not the products of creative leisure, like other great works of art. They were born in the heat of argument; they are weapons of verbal warfare. Hounded by critics who found fault with His every utterance, Jesus frequently silenced His opposition with a good story. P. G. Wodehouse has one of his characters describe Jesus' ammunition. No theologian has phrased it better. "A parable . . . is one of those stories in the Bible which sounds at first like a pleasant yarn, but keeps something up its sleeve which suddenly pops out and knocks you flat."

May you be knocked flat! I have been, and am better for it.

Here are three suggestions for your reading:

1) Read each story for its central truth. Don't be sidetracked by minor elements that may be fascinating but are beside the point. Your question is always, "What *one* statement is Jesus making here?"

Don't push for hidden meanings. The early church father Tertullian offers a good bad example. In the story of the prodigal son, he tells us the elder son is the Jew, the younger is the Christian. The inheritance he asks for is the knowledge of God which every person has as his birthright. The person who hires him in the far country is the devil; the robe his father gives him on his return home is the sonship that Adam lost in the beginning of human history. The ring stands for baptism, the feast for the Lord's Supper, and the fatted calf for Christ himself.

It's fun to turn your imagination loose like this, but it isn't fair. Let the parable tell its own story and make its own point.

2) Take note of the circumstances in which Jesus tells the story. They often help you to find His purpose more quickly. Read the verses before and following or, if necessary, the chapter before and following.

3) Become involved. Jesus spoke two thousand years ago, but He didn't stop there. He still speaks through His Word. The parables are for you and me. "What's in this for me?" is always a proper question in these studies. When you ask it, Jesus will speak to you about God's will for your life, about your accountability before the Father, about living a compassionate, watchful, productive life. You'll know more fully what it is to be a citizen in the kingdom of God. You'll be like the good soil in the parable of the sower. You'll produce!

I. COME TO THE PARTY

Luke 14:16-24

"I've been invited to lunch at the White House."

My friend was ecstatic. The President of the United States was inviting several Christian leaders from around the nation to lunch at the White House. He wanted their advice on some proposed legislation he would soon be sending to Congress. My friend was one of the chosen. Nothing could stand in the way of that invitation. He was going!

Most of us would feel the same way. Who in his right mind would turn down an invitation to the White House?

Or to the Palace? If you lived in a kingdom, an invitation from the king could hardly be refused.

It's a king's request that Jesus speaks of in the parable of the wedding feast. Luke calls the host simply "a certain man," but Matthew's version says he is "a king who prepared a wedding banquet for his son." Jesus speaks of a king and a wedding feast: an invitation from the *most important person* in the kingdom to attend the *most important event* of the kingdom.

The food alone would make attending worthwhile. The typical diet of the day was vegetarian. Occasionally some fish would be added, and very infrequently a little goat meat. The meat of cattle and oxen was a rare treat, reserved for special occasions—like this wedding feast, for instance. The invited guests would dine like royalty!

To just such a feast Jesus compares the kingdom of God. The king's summons to the wedding celebration is like Jesus' invitation to enter the kingdom of God. As improper as this language may sound, Jesus' call to discipleship is, among other things, God's invitation for us to come to His party.

The party isn't for everyone. The king will not force anybody to attend against his will.

THE CELEBRATION IS FOR
THOSE WHO ACCEPT THE INVITATION

The surprise in Jesus' parable is that the guests reject the invitation. They had already been formally invited earlier. Then they were informed that as soon as everything was ready, the king's servants would be sent to fetch them. The guests weren't caught off guard. Their refusal now, after receiving the earlier invitation, could only be interpreted as a deliberate snub.

They sent their regrets instead. And their excuses.

Such flimsy excuses. A newly purchased field to check out: would a man have bought it sight unseen? Having to test a yoke of oxen: surely the oxen were in no hurry to be put to the test. A recent marriage: perhaps a little more reasonable excuse, but still lacking in real urgency. Each excuse says the same thing: "My own affairs are more important than the king's party." Jesus' meaning is clear: the guests consider God's affairs to be less compelling than their own.

No doubt Jesus narrates this tale to rebuke His own nation, Israel. For centuries, God has been preparing His people for a coming celebration. A Savior is coming from God himself; the Savior will announce the kingdom of God and will bring grace and truth. He will save His people from their sins. He will be like the servant announcing that all preparations are in order for the king's party. Instead of an eager welcome, however, the Savior Jesus is suffering the same arrogant rejection as the king's servant, and from the very ones for whom the party has been prepared.

In place of acceptance, they send excuses. On the surface, they may seem plausible enough, perhaps, even though lacking in urgency. Business matters, family concerns. They still rank at the top of the list of most popular rationalizations we come up with when we'd rather not be bothered by God's requests.

Tony Twist, youth minister at the East Ninety-first Street Christian Church in Indianapolis, published the results of his whimsical poll of the most popular excuses church members give him. "What is your favorite excuse?" he asks them,

"When you don't want to date some 'turkey'?"
   Mother wants me to stay home with the family.
"When you don't want to help a friend in need?"
   I've got to be at home with the wife.
"When you don't want to teach a Sunday School class?"
   We're out of town visiting family a lot.
"When you don't want to help in V.B.S.?"
   Vacation with family.
"When you want to avoid any commitment?"
   Family.

Then Twist muses on the giants of the faith who gave up their families for the cause of Christ, naming Jesus himself, Paul, Peter, St. Frances, Thomas Merton, and C. S. Lewis among them.[1] Christians are seldom required to choose between family duties and the call of the kingdom, but when that choice has to be made, discipleship demands obedience to God's summons. To do otherwise is to make an idol of the family.

The same is true of business. God understands our need to earn a living, of course. We can't expect Him to approve, however, our worship of the dollar. Clovis Chappell told this story many years ago. I repeat it because its moral is timeless. Chappell was standing in front of the First National Bank one day, talking with its president, who was also the superintendent of their church's Sunday School. The man must have been feeling some guilt pangs, because before his pastor could say anything he confessed, "Preacher, I won't be with you tomorrow." He offered his excuse, and Chappell said nothing.

"You don't see anything wrong in that, do you?" he demanded.

"Do you?" the preacher returned his question.

"Well, I suppose that it is not exactly what a practicing Christian ought to do, but you preachers don't understand. A man must live."[2]

He sounds just like the men in Jesus' story, doesn't he? A man must live. He must examine his field, he must test his oxen, and he must attend his wife. His family comes first; his business is his priority. God gets what's left over.

Jesus does not so much condemn as grieve for those who miss the party. They have missed their opportunity. "All great events hang by a single thread. The clever man takes advantage of everything, neglects nothing that may give him some added opportunity." Even the cynical Napoleon Bonaparte, writing the above to Talleyrand in 1797, knew that the difference between greatness and mediocrity is often in one's ability to seize the moment without delay. It will probably not pass this way again.

In May of 1979, when American Airlines Flight 191 crashed shortly after takeoff from Chicago's O'Hare Airport, I lost one of my close friends. Carol Ferntheil and I had worked together in Christian publishing. When she died, I could recall many rich hours together. We had loved and respected each other as fellow Christians and as comrades in a cause, and we had said so. My loss was easier to bear than that of a sobbing father whose eighteen-year-old daughter had gone down on the same plane. "The one thing about this that makes it so hard,'" he said when he was told of her death, "is that I never told her I loved her. I was so busy and always intended to but she grew up so fast there just never seemed to be time."[3] He had lost his opportunity. He had had fields to examine and oxen to test.

Remember three things come not back;
The arrow sent upon its track—
It will not swerve, it will not stay
Its speed: it flies to wound, or slay.
The spoken word so often forgot
By thee; but it has perished not;
In other hearts 'tis living still
And doing work for good or ill.
And *the lost opportunity*
That cometh back no more to thee.
In vain thou weepest, in vain dost yearn,
Those three will nevermore return.

Jesus does not castigate the refusing guests as evil men. Their fault is not that they are bad, but preoccupied. Judgment falls not upon the too bad alone, but also upon the "too busy."

ONLY THOSE WHO ARE NOT TOO BUSY TO APPRECIATE THE HONOR WILL ATTEND

They recognize what the invitation is worth. They are grateful for being unexpectedly selected by their king.

Since those who might think they have every right to be invited (like the Israelites who boasted that only they were the true people of God) have devalued the invitation, the host turns to persons who would never expect to be at his table. They are the poor, the infirm, the outsiders, the humble people who know their place and keep it. What a thrill for them to be in the presence of the great one. They quickly accept.

How often God uses people you would least expect to be chosen. A Moses who stammers, leading the nation to freedom. A poor shepherd like Amos, rising to eminence among the great spokesmen of God. A baby born in a manger, becoming the Savior of mankind. A John Bunyan, who described his father's house as "being of that rank that is meanest and most despised of all the families in the land," writing one of history's most widely read books (Pilgrim's Progress). A Gideon, who sounds like Bunyan as he says, "My clan is the weakest in Manasseh, and I am the least in my family," leading his hand-picked army of God's warriors to victory.

God seems to rely on the least among us because the greatest are too busy—or too sure of themselves—to grab the moment of opportunity. They don't always discern what a boon is being offered them. Robert Heller in his Great Executive Dream[4] has some fun at the expense of "those unsung ghosts of American business" who deliberately and with blindness aforethought passed up opportunities to make a fortune, men like

the IBM man who turned down the Univac computer,
the Du Pont executive who showed the inventor of
    xerography the door, or
the Kodak man who turned up his nose at Polaroid.
These losers, Heller adds, belong in the company of persons who scoffed at the future of the horseless carriage. It isn't, he adds, that they were afraid to take risks; they just didn't recognize opportunity when they saw it.

One of the most famous of these bad judges of good chances was Mark Twain, who squandered a fortune in harebrained schemes that led him to financial ruin, but with steady strength of mind firmly rejected an appeal from a poor but brilliant inventor who asked him to invest only $500 in his invention in exchange for as large a share in the new company as Twain wanted. Twain saw no future in the contraption, so he sent Alexander Graham Bell on his way. To Bell and his telephone Twain forever said good-by to the incredible fortune he could have made.

Missed opportunities. The greatest of them all is the invitation to live forever in the presence of God. To fritter away your life on fields or oxen or even the routine duties of marriage when you could be feasting on the abundance of God's eternal party is to throw away the chance of a lifetime—or rather, the chance of an eternity! Jesus' moral is clear: don't be too busy for God!

GOD WILL KEEP TRYING
UNTIL HIS HOUSE IS FULL

We are somewhat surprised by the host's *unexpected importunity*. He is determined to have his house filled. He dispatches his servants with orders to "make them come in." He senses that "the poor, the crippled, the blind and the lame" will be reluctant to come to the great man's home. All their lives they have been despised as rejects and failures. They have been forced to cower in corners because they can't compete in a society that has no patience for the handicapped. How can they trust this servant? How will they know this is not another cruel joke? Will they go as told, only to be rebuffed at the gate? Who has ever been so kind to them before?

The host's insistence does seem a little strange, but it is very much in harmony with everything the Bible teaches about God's desire that the whole world should be saved. In the Old Testament, from Genesis through Malachi, God's Word repeats the theme that God is a loving Lord who wants to bless the world through His chosen ones (see Genesis 12:1-3). The good news about Jesus is that God so loved the whole world (John 3:16) that He sent His Son to seek everywhere—even "into the streets and alleys of the town" and "the roads and country lanes"—to save the lost.

This parable has to be studied with the Great Commission (Matthew 28:18-20). It is also in harmony with Jesus' first commission, the disciples' practice mission to Israel (Matthew 10:5-8). Even then Jesus sent them to "heal the sick, raise the dead, cleanse those who have leprosy,[and] drive out demons." When John the Baptist requested proof that Jesus was the Messiah, Jesus gave His credentials as follows: "The blind receive sight, the lame walk, those who have leprosy are cured, the deaf hear, the dead are raised, and the good news is preached to the poor" (Matthew 11:5, 6). The Lord's party is for the ones who least expect to be invited. And God *urges* them to attend. They have nothing to fear. This is no joke. They, so hardened to daily abuse, are the very ones God especially wants. He will receive and take care of them. They, too, will celebrate.

Their reason for rejoicing is not primarily because He meets their physical needs, however. What causes their abundant joy is that He has sought them out. *He* has come to *them*. Some Bible commentators suggest that in the parable, the residents "of the town" could refer to the poor and sinful of Israel, and those in "the roads and country lanes" could indicate the Gentiles. Whether this reading is correct or not, what is inescapable is the host's compulsion that even the least desirable person should know he is welcome.

God's sense of urgency has frequently stood in direct contrast to the complacency of His people. In a ministers' meeting in Northampton, England, in 1786, William Carey, the preacher-cobbler from Moulton, asked, "Do the brethren not think that the command given by our Lord to the Apostles to teach all nations is obligatory on all succeeding ministers to the end of the world, seeing that the accompanying promise is of equal extent?"

The chairman scolded Carey, even shouted at him. "You are a miserable enthusiast for asking such a question. Certainly nothing can be done before another Pentecost, when an effusion of miraculous gifts, including the gift of tongues, will give effect to the commission of Christ as at first." So the ministers satisfied themselves that they had no need to do anything "in the roads and country lanes." If God wanted to do anything about the lost, He'd have to pull off another Day of Pentecost (Acts 2). Until then, they would let the lost be lost.

Carey couldn't stand it. He felt he had to practice what he preached. His decision took him to India, where he shoved open the door on modern missions. Try as he might, he could see no way to excuse himself from the imperative of the Great Commission. God's banquet table was not yet filled. There were still other outcasts to be invited to the party.

We would do an injustice to this parable if we ignored the final warning of judgment: "I tell you, not one of those men who were invited will get a taste of my banquet."

To refuse to attend is to be left out of the celebration. You can't have it both ways: you can't prefer your personal business to the Lord's and still expect to enjoy His party. Your place at the table will be taken by others. C. S. Lewis has summarized the whole matter in *The Great Divorce:*

"There are only two kinds of people in the end: those who say to God, 'Thy will be done,' and those to whom God says, in the end, '*Thy* will be done.' "

It is Lewis' opinion that "all that are in Hell, choose it." They refuse the invitation.

"Without that self-choice there could be no Hell. No soul that seriously and constantly desires joy will ever miss it. Those who seek find. To those who knock it is opened."[5]

To miss Heaven, Lewis insists, is to have preferred Hell. To choose fields or oxen or wife over God is to get what you prefer.

Don't miss the party.

NOTES

[1]*The 91st Edition,* May 29, 1981, p. 2.

[2]*Meet These Men* (New York, Nashville: Abingdon Press, 1956), pp. 44, 45.

[3]Quoted by Ray Jones, *Clearwater Christian* (June 13, 1979), p. 4.

[4]Robert Heller, *The Great Executive Dream* (New York: Dell Publishing, 1974), p. 170.

[5]C.S. Lewis, *The Great Divorce* (New York: MacMillan, 1964), pp. 72, 73.

II. THE REASON FOR THE PARTY

Luke 15

When World Vision rescued 238 Vietnamese fleeing from the Communists in their homeland, not everybody cheered. Operation Seasweep plucked these brave but frightened refugees out of cold waters of desperation. You would think the whole world would have praised World Vision. Some cynics in the media, however, raised the predictable question: "Was it worth it?"[1]

Perhaps you could argue that it was a fair question. USA government officials advised World Vision to do what they themselves were doing: ignore the problem. Some 8,000 to 10,000 refugees were fleeing Vietnam every month, they said, and less than half of them were actually making it to freedom. No rescue operation could save all these people, so why try to save any of them? Such is the counsel of the worldly wise.

In hard cash, World Vision's donors paid $1,300 for every person rescued. That really isn't very much, is it, to save a human being? Surely these persons were worth $1,300 apiece.

But what if the cost had been $50,000 each? Would these Vietnamese refugees have been worth that much?

Or maybe $5,000,000? In that same year (1978), Adam Starchild, president of the Minerva Consulting Group, added up the value of human biochemicals from chemical specialty company catalogs. He included such things as hemoglobin ($2.95 a gram) and the female hormone prolactin ($17,500,000 a gram). He concluded that every human being is worth $6,000,000—and that was in 1978 dollars![2] Using Starchild's figures, then, we can declare Operation Seasweep a whopping financial success, returning a $6,000,000 value for every $1,300 invested!

It seems pretty crass, doesn't it, to discuss human beings in these monetary terms? To a money-mad age like ours, though, nothing else quite makes the point. Maybe we need to pin a price-tag on every individual to remind society that persons have value. I like what famed American educator Horace Mann said to his audience as he dedicated a recreation home for boys. "If all the money and energy you have expended result in the salvation of only one boy, they will not have been in vain."

Later one of the contributors challenged him. "My dear Mr.

Mann, weren't you exaggerating a bit when you said all our expenditure would be worthwhile if we save just *one* boy?"

"Not if it were my boy," Mann replied.

There is something Christlike in that answer. When the religious leaders fussed about Jesus' disregard of social etiquette, He told them some stories of the importance of human lives. His opponents may have criticized Him for hobnobbing and eating with "tax collectors and 'sinners,' " but that is because they didn't use God's scales to weigh the worth of every human being. The parable of the lost sheep, like those of the lost coin and the lost son (also in Luke 15), demonstrates how God's scales work. All three are about the loss of something very valuable—and the celebration that took place when it was found.

LOST

No shepherd worth the name can shrug off the loss of a sheep. He could never say, "Oh, well, even though one is missing, I still have the other ninety-nine." A good shepherd knows his sheep by name; he protects them from every danger and, if necessary, lays down his life for his sheep (John 10:1-18). When he discovers that one is missing, he immediately sets out to rescue it.

A good shepherd is like the God in whom Jesus taught us to believe. He also notices a missing one. He is even more observant: He counts the hairs of the head (Matthew 10:30), He clothes the lilies of the field (Matthew 6:30), and He feeds the birds of the air (Matthew 6:26). Certainly He of whom Peter would write, "The Lord is not slow in keeping his promise, as some understand slowness. He is patient with you, not wanting anyone to perish . . . "(2 Peter 3:9), has given every indication of the value He places on human life. One does not easily allow something or someone of value to slip away unnoticed.

Jesus' respect for the dignity of every human being is still not popular everywhere. More in tune with the prevailing opinion on university campuses, for example, is this note sounded by historian Carl Becker:

Man is but a foundling in the cosmos, abandoned by forces that created him. Unparented, unassisted and undirected by omniscient or benevolent authority, he must fend for himself, and with the aid of his own limited intelligence find his way about in an indifferent universe.[3]

A cheerful opinion! Man—the final product of natural developments that just chanced to happen. Man lost—because there is no One to find him. Man worthless—because there is no One to value him. Man insignificant—because he measures his height against the stars in the heavens. He is nothing, he concludes, an inconsequential speck on a third-rate planet in a minor galaxy of an immeasurable universe. He is nothing and he is lost.

The whole human race—lost.

But that is not the whole story, not by a long shot. It is true that, astronomically speaking, man is insignificant. But it is also true, as someone has wisely countered, "Astronomically speaking, man is the astronomer." The astronomer knows the stars; do the stars know the astronomer? Is greatness to be measured in light years or space miles or mass volume alone? May we not instead speak of awareness and the capacity to know and understand and consciously change and produce change? Pascal, whom I never tire of quoting, sums it up for me: "Man is but a reed, the weakest in nature, but he is a thinking reed."

And he is worth saving.

SOUGHT AND FOUND

The three parables of Luke 15 diverge here. The shepherd goes after the lost sheep, the woman searches diligently for her lost coin, but the loving father of the prodigal son must stay at home. His heart searches for his son, but his body must abide until the wayward boy comes to himself and returns. Love cannot force a reconciliation. The father may yearn for his son to be with him, but first must come the son's independence. Only then the reunion.

The father's heart must have hurt unbearably. The separation was bad enough, but the fear that something might happen to prevent his boy's return was even worse. Daily the father's eyes scoured the horizon for a sign, any sign, that the son was found and was returning to his home. The waiting was like a cross.

The cross of Christ is the Father's cross also, poised there between Heaven and earth, a constant reminder of the extent to which our Father has gone in His waiting search for us.

It is an agony many loving parents know. The mother of a certain ten-year-old daughter knows of it. All her life, the little girl had been afflicted with some mysterious malady. Every year this something took hold of her. The effect was frightening. Ordinarily she was bright, even brilliant. Musically gifted, socially at ease, and a leader in her class, she would suddenly become uncoordinated, reclusive, and given to daydreams from which it was difficult to recall her. Her grades dropped, her handwriting deteriorated into a nearly illegible scrawl. Occasionally she would faint or complain of strange pains or numbness in her arms or legs.

Doctors were mystified. From specialist to specialist her mother took her, repeating her story, submitting her to yet another battery of tests, suffering again as the doctors told her, as if reading from the same script, that they could find nothing wrong. They could detect no physical cause of the illness. They even doubted the seriousness of her problem. They seemed to agree that if a problem really existed, it was in the neurotically overprotective mother and not in the child.

In despair the mother cried to her minister, "All I want is to have my sweet little girl back." She continued her search, in spite of the disappointments and implied ridicule. Finally, the elusive physical cause was found—by the mother, not the doctors. With proper diet she combatted her girl's severe food allergies, and she got her "sweet little girl back."

Hers is not an unusual story. It could be told by parents everywhere who have lost a child one way or another. Love drives them to any extreme in order to rescue their loved one. It is of the essence of parental love to seek and find. This is also the Heavenly Father's character.

These parables speak, then, of the persistence of God's love and His estimate of human worth. The sheep is worth the effort the shepherd expends to find it; the coin is precious to the poor woman who loses it; and the son is valuable beyond reckoning to the father seeking his return.

These stories need to be relearned by every generation, ours perhaps more than most. In a century that has witnessed the slaughter of more people than in any other in history, it is obvious that mankind generally considers individual human beings to be quite expendable. Stalin, Hitler, Amin, Khomeini—the list seems almost endless—are latter-day incarnations of Shakespeare's cynical Falstaff, who recruited a ragtag company of society's dregs to fight his Prince's war, then contemptuously called the pitiful rascals "food for powder, food for powder," and dismissed them with, "They'll fill a pit as well as better. Tush, man, mortal men, mortal men."[4] Shakespeare wrote in the sixteenth and seventeenth centuries, but things haven't changed —mortal men are still filling bloody pits because people in high places haven't yet come to Jesus' appreciation of individual human worth.

Perhaps it is because they are not sure of their own worth. They may be like the young college student who told his counselor that when he got in touch with himself through meditation, he discovered that he was not worth knowing.

At the opposite pole is the famous Muhammed Ali, who fashioned his singular lack of humility into an unmistakable trademark. No one living in America in the '60s and '70s could have missed Ali's proclamation: "I am the greatest!" His boasts made good press and may even have convinced a few. He gave his inner insecurity away, though, when he announced he was changing his name from Cassius Clay to Muhammed Ali because he didn't want "nobody" to call him by his slave name "no more."

Even if Ali were right, even if he could convince himself that he was the greatest, can the rest of us use self-hypnosis as effectively? What about those who haven't become world champion boxers or world champion anything else? We hold down forty-hour a week jobs, rear a couple of kids, live in modest houses in modest communities and are treated with modest respect. Does this sound like "the greatest"? What are *we* worth?

Look again at Jesus' description of the Good Shepherd in John 10:3. "He calls his own sheep by name. . . ." Then verse 11: "The good shepherd lays down his life for the sheep." Now verse 14: "I know my sheep and my sheep know me."

Add to these some verses from the Old Testament. In Exodus 33:17, the Lord says, "I know you by name." Here is Isaiah 45:3, 4:

"I will give you the treasures of darkness,
    riches stored in secret places,
so that you may know that I am the Lord,
    the God of Israel, *who calls you by name.*
For the sake of Jacob my servant,
    of Israel my chosen,
I call you by name
    and bestow on you a title of honor. . . ."

The day will come, Isaiah promises, when God will redeem His lost people and give them a new name:

21

"For Zion's sake I will not keep silent,
    for Jerusalem's sake I will not remain quiet,
till her righteousness shines out like the dawn,
    her salvation like a blazing torch.
The nations will see your righteousness,
    and all kings your glory;
you will be called by a new name
    that the mouth of the Lord will bestow (Isaiah 62:1, 2).

The Bible lays repeated stress on the importance of names. The genealogies in Genesis, Matthew, and Luke are examples. They testify that nowhere in the Bible is man—any man or woman—treated as a cog in a machine or as "food for powder." All persons are flesh and blood, made in the image of God, creatures formed by the loving handiwork of God. And every one has a name. Everybody is a somebody.

Everybody has a name because someone thought him important enough to give him one, to distinguish him from all the rest of humanity. When my wife and I named our children, we thought long and hard about each one. We debated, we discussed, we even disagreed, then we named them what *she* thought they should be called! But each name was chosen with care, because each child was special to us. We bestowed worth, if you please, when we named them. That, says Isaiah, is what God has done for His people as well.

The apostle Paul says the same thing: "For this reason I kneel before the Father, *from whom his whole family* in heaven and on earth *derives its name* . . ." Ephesians 3:14. God created us, God named us, and God bestowed worth on us. He made us somebodies. To Him, we are "the greatest."

CELEBRATED

It is no wonder, is it then, that when the lost becomes found, there is a party? A priceless one has been recovered. That is cause for celebration:

"I tell you that in the same way there is more rejoicing in heaven over one sinner who repents than over ninety-nine righteous persons who do not need to repent" (Luke 15:7; cf. v. 10)

Jesus still has the "tax collectors and sinners" in mind. They may be lost, but only temporarily. The can repent (turn again toward God) as surely as the lost son returned home to his father. Then the singing on earth will be amplified by the angelic chorus. Someone of infinite value has been saved!

In Chapter 1, we studied Jesus' invitation to the festivities. Now, after looking at the stories in Luke 15, we understand a little more of the reasons Jesus likens the kingdom of God to a party. First, because of the incalculable value of the persons who enter God's kingdom. Second, because of the unrelenting love of the finder. It takes at least two to celebrate. When the seeker and the sought have come together, their relief and joy are immeasurable. Their emotions spill over into singing. They can't help sharing their joy with each other and with all their loved ones. "Rejoice with me" is the natural consequence of a successful search. The only appropriate activity is some kind of party.

As my family and I were about to leave our pastorate in Indianapolis to move to Arizona, I had to decline an invitation that I really wanted to accept. The party was a "Gospel Hoedown." Rick and Becky were inviting their new Christian friends over for an evening of singing and fellowship. Twenty-four people crowded into their house and the singing lasted until late in the evening. I knew better than to attend. There was no way I could join in the singing and then preach three times the next morning.

It was a new kind of party for the young couple. They hadn't been Christians very long. She had hardly ever been inside a church building when we first met, just a few months before. I went to their home because they desperately needed to talk to someone. A month earlier, Becky's brother had been killed in an automobile accident. Ever since, she had been trying to find someone who could talk to her about death—and about God.

Actually, two brothers were involved. They had moved in with Rick and Becky from their home in Georgia. Country kids in a strange and wonderful city, these teenagers soon found a crowd that spelled no good for them. In a wild night of drinking and drugs, their car went out of control and crashed. One of the brothers was seriously wounded. The other was killed.

Becky had a thousand questions. She also bore a crushing load of guilt. If only she had done this, or had not done that. You can imagine how she felt. We talked. We talked about God's love and His forgiveness, about our sin and need for that forgiveness. We talked for hours.

The next morning, they were in worship. At the end of the sermon, when I invited the worshipers to accept Christ, they walked down the aisle. They were baptized into Christ and His body. Once they had felt desperately lost. Now they were found.

You see why they *had* to throw a party?

You see how the kingdom of God *is* like a party?

We have reason to celebrate. God has told us that, in His opinion, *we* are the reason to celebrate.

NOTES

[1]Reported in *World Vision* (Vol. 22, No. 12, Dec., 1978), p. 2.

[2]*Saturday Review* (October 28, 1978), p. 6.

[3]Quoted in William L. Shirer, *20th Century Journey* (New York: Simon and Schuster, 1976), p. 11.

[4]*King Henry IV, Part I,* IV, ii.

III. LISTEN FOR A CHANGE

Matthew 13:1-23

"I don't know where you are coming from."
"You never listen to me."
"I hear you, but I don't know what you're saying."
"What we have here is a failure to communicate."
Communication. Nothing is more vital in human relationships and nothing is harder to achieve. Failure to communicate is a leading cause of divorce, of corporation mismanagement, of church fights, and of just about any other group breakdown you can mention. "I don't know where you are coming from" may offend an English teacher's ears, but it is a pretty accurate diagnosis of the problem. Communication is complex. Two people may use the same words but mean totally different things by them, because of "where they are coming from." If we could get ourselves out of the way and just let the words pass between us, there would be no problem. But we can't remove ourselves.

GOOD COMMUNICATION REQUIRES A SENDER AND A RECEIVER

When we talk to each other, we unwittingly charge our language with
—our unspoken fears
—our undiscerned prejudices
—our dominating ego needs, both conscious and subconscious
—our social values, the yardsticks we use to measure whether our conversation is with one equal, superior, or inferior to ourselves
—our experiences
—our personal hopes, dreams, and expectations
—our assessment of the other speaker: social standing, intelligence, character, personality, knowledge of the subject, religious and moral convictions, and everything else that matters to us
—and more.

RECEIVERS ARE LIKE SOIL

In Jesus' usual, profoundly simple manner, He captures the incredible complexity of the listening process by comparing a hearer to a type of soil. Good seed can be counted on; it will take root and produce in hospitable soil. It will fail to produce in a hostile or unreceptive environment. In this case, crop failure is not the fault of the sower or the seed, but the soil.

For this reason, Jesus says, when a sower goes out to sow, he knows in advance that much seed will be wasted. The first-century Palestinian farmer first sows the seed on top of the ground, then plows the seed under. The harvest will vary according to the readiness of the soil.

Some seeds will fall on the path. Before they can penetrate the hard surface, birds will snatch them for food. The Word of God has similar difficulty when it falls on hardened hearts. Its rejection is immediate. There is no communication.

Dwight L. Moody was so successful a preacher we forget that even he could not convert all his hearers. He wished for power to make men understand that God really loves them. If they could just receive that message, "how we should find them crowding into the kingdom of heaven! The trouble is that men think God hates them; and so they are all the time running away from Him."[1] Hardened. Misinformed. Unable to hear the truth. When Moody built his church in Chicago, he decided that if he couldn't preach this truth into his hearers' hearts, he would try visual aids. He ordered gas-jets installed above his pulpit, spelling the words GOD IS LOVE with them. He wanted no one to miss the message. More than once the sign worked where the sermon failed.

But no matter what gimmick you use, some people simply will not hear the Word.

Others will receive it but, flighty and shallow in character, they will not retain the message, like rocky soil that prevents seed from taking root. For a moment they seem to understand and want to obey. Then the flicker of truth is extinguished and they hurry off to something else, titillated by the fad of the moment, captivated by the lights and sounds of the popular imagination. The promise of new life in the Word is just that—promise, but without delivery.

In his *African Diary*, Helmut Thielicke tells of a poignant encounter he has with one of the ship's sailors, far gone in his cups, pouring out his soul to Thielicke because "you're a priest or something." Alcohol has lowered his inhibitions so that he can talk about himself, but has drugged his brain beyond the point of intelligent conversation. Thielicke asks him for another chance to talk tomorrow, hoping then to make sense of the man's words. But they never talk again. The sailor avoids him, embarrassed that he has opened himself to a stranger. The moment of his openness to a word of truth is gone. Thielicke concludes that this is a common happening. When sailors (and passengers as well) are sober, they are closed and defensive; when drunk, they open up and their long-repressed feelings burst forth and their minds are receptive to truth. Then sobriety returns on the morrow and they become defensive once more, shutting off any real communication.

For a moment, there seems to be hope. Only for a moment, though. The soil is too rocky, the opening too shallow.

Some sincere believers would like to receive the Word. But there are thorns. They have a hard time concentrating. Their worries intrude. They are easily distracted, their other responsibilities clamor for attention. They want to say with Samuel, "Speak, for your servant is listening" (1 Samuel 3:10), and they really are listening, for a while. They answer, they listen, but they can't concentrate because something else is calling, and they want to listen to that, too.

To concentrate is to discriminate. To concentrate on the Word of God is to block out other words. It is to hear God and no other before Him. The people of Israel understood something of the exclusive demand of the Word of God. They said to Moses, "Speak to us yourself and we will listen. But do not have God speak to us or we will die" (Exodus 20:19).

They were right. When God speaks—and we really listen—we are dead to anything else, even our own voice. We know that when we hear Him, we must heed Him. To hear God is to obey God and no other. "We must obey God rather than men!" (Acts 5:29). It is one thing to listen to Moses or another of God's servants; we may even try to dismiss their words, if we want to, as merely the reasonings of men. But we cannot so dismiss a "thus saith the Lord." So we choose not to listen; we prefer our distractions.

We are the losers. Jesus rightly calls us thorny soil. We are pricked by the thorns of worry and distraction and in the end must plant a self-fashioned crown of thorns on our brows. We crucify ourselves, but not the truth.

We lose because there is no word like God's Word. Listening to no other speaker will produce in us such fruitful living, such honest character, such joy. His Word keeps us from sinning against Him; it fills its hearer with grace and truth. It judges and corrects our conduct while helping us fulfill our potential. Without it, we yield an impure harvest.

What Shakespeare's publishers said of his plays could be far more appropriately said of God's Word. John Heminge and Henrie Condell appointed themselves the guardians and publishers of the great dramatist's manuscripts. Shakespeare had treated his plays with incredible carelessness, preparing them for immediate production without much thought to posterity. Heminge and Condell gathered the plays into a magnificent folio edition, which they published after Shakespeare's death. In their preface, they paid tribute to his genius:

"Read him, therefore; and again, and again: And if you do not like him, surely you are in some manifest danger, not to understand him."[2]

The fault is in the reader, not the writer. Just as certainly, "you are in some manifest danger" not to receive the seed of God's Word and let it grow and be nurtured in your being.

GOOD RECEIVERS REALLY SEE AND HEAR

Jesus' disciples, the Scripture suggests, are like the good soil. They have received "the knowledge of the secrets of the kingdom of heaven" (Matthew 13:11).

"Blessed are your eyes because they see, and your ears because they hear. For I tell you the truth, many prophets and righteous men longed to see what you see but did not see it, and to hear what you hear but did not hear it" (Matthew 13:16, 17).

The disciples are good soil because they have prepared themselves to hear and receive Jesus' Word. They have left home and career; they have forsaken their secure traditions and comfortable routines. They have come to Jesus fully. They devote themselves to Him and His instruction. When He sends them out to preach and minister to their countrymen, they obey. When He calls them to follow, they follow. There is nothing casual about their listening. They concentrate.

In their quickness to learn, they differ markedly from the people Isaiah describes:

"Though seeing, they do not see;

though hearing, they do not hear or understand" (Matthew 13:13).

It is possible to take God for granted, especially if you believe you are His only chosen people. When He speaks, then, you can pretend to hear without really hearing, and you can claim to see what you have not seen. You don't fool God, though; you only dull your sensitivities and shut out His truth.

The disciples, on the contrary, are blessed of eye and ear because they are really seeing and hearing.

Jesus' simple story makes us face up to the status of our communication with God, doesn't it? He has sown the seed and has made His Word available to us in print. If something is amiss, it is not the fault of the Sower or the Seed. Perhaps we have not proved ourselves the best soil.

A discouragingly large number of Christians have not taken advantage of the printed Word. A famous examination was given a few years ago to high school juniors and seniors. Some of the tested students believed Sodom and Gomorrah were lovers, that Matthew, Mark, Luther, and John wrote the Gospels, and that Eve was created from an apple. Perhaps Charles Schulz had this test in mind when he had his Peppermint Patty tell Charlie Brown that she wanted to study religion so she could learn about "Moses, and St. Paul and Minneapolis."

What must we do to *hear* God's word? At the least, we must *concentrate, commit* ourselves, and *apply* Biblical teaching.

Concentration

A hundred years ago, young G. Campbell Morgan, who later became a world-renowned Baptist minister, was torn by doubts about the Bible's truth. He realized that he had spent too much time studying about the Bible without really learning what was in the Bible. So he locked up his scholarly studies about the Bible in order to concentrate on listening to God's Word alone. He had some doubts; he knew that his father may have been wrong in claiming the Bible to be the Word of God. But of this he was certain: if it were the Word of God, and if he approached it with an open and unprejudiced mind, it would be able to give sufficient assurance with no other assistance needed.

It was and it did.

To concentrate is to banish distractions. It is to become so absorbed in the subject that you lose yourself and become a slave to the dictates of the one speaking—thus liberating yourself from captivity to your own ego. In a remarkable passage in Pasternak's *Dr. Zhivago,* the hero muses on the paradox that in a Communist society, freedom exists only in concentration camps. It is a truth at the heart of the Christian faith, also. True freedom comes to the imprisoned, true life to those who have died, true productivity to those who concentrate. Only when the ego does not distract are you prepared to hear the truth.

That grand old man of twentieth-century Christian missions, John R. Mott, made this his goal in *Confronting Young Men with the Living Christ.*

"If I might share with you my dearest wish it is that by the time I come to my old age I may have so brought all thoughts into obedience to His marvellous captivity, that whenever my mind comes out of unconsciousness into consciousness it will revert naturally and inevitably to Jesus Christ."[3]

It is in the Bible that one meets Jesus Christ and in study of the Bible that one really hears His voice. If you honestly want to hear the Word of God and receive it, Bible study is no irksome duty prescribed by the preacher, but is instead a dialogue between Speaker and listener in which the Word of God comes alive and speaks with human voice. And a human heart responds.

Commitment

Concentration demands commitment. It is not easy to listen when there is so much static. Jesus may stand at the door and knock (Revelation 3:20), but the sound is nearly lost in the cacophony of poundings at our heart. We'll never hear, in fact, until we make a conscious decision to listen, to strain to hear this knocking above all knockings and to this teaching above all other teachings.

Bible study, like much else about the Christian walk, can never be a casual affair. No important conversation is relaxed. Everything about you is alert, eager, ready to respond, seeking more information, wanting more insight, leaning forward to catch every tone and overtone. If there is one thing our so-called age of anxiety should have taught us, it is that peace and joy forever elude us until we are surprised by them as a result of our commitment to Someone higher than even peace and joy. The Lord's blessings come to him who has first made Him Lord; only to them is He Lord.

"For to me, to live is Christ," is the way the apostle Paul describes his commitment (Philippians 1:21). Every real achiever could pray with Andre Gide, "O Lord, permit me to want only one thing and to want it constantly."[4] Every true lover learns quickly that there is no real communication in conversation without commitment to the loved one and concentration on the loved one's words.

Application

"Do not merely listen to the word, and so deceive yourselves. Do what it says" (James 1:22). The act of listening is not completed when the sound waves beat against the eardrum. That is just a sensory achievement. Biblically speaking, to hear means to heed—to do. My father understood this meaning. "Do you hear me?" was his way of demanding action. He wasn't asking whether the sound waves had arrived; he was looking for the *doing* that should follow the *hearing*.

Scripture study is more than an amassing of interesting facts about Bible people or places. It has nothing to do with the notable feat of the man who "studied" the King James Version of the Bible. He announced that he found 773,693 words. As if that weren't impressive enough, he said that they contained 3,539,489 letters. Interesting, but highly irrelevant.

I am more impressed with the method of Juan Carlos Ortiz. A few years ago, he and I were roommates at a retreat for college students for which we were both speaking. During the weekend, he tantalized me with many of his insights into the Christian faith, but what impressed me most was his description of the method he adopted to help his people really *hear* God's Word.

He questioned the value of speaking every week on one subject in the sermon, another in Sunday School class, and yet a third at the mid-week prayer meeting. He decided to preach just one sermon on one subject until he saw his people actually doing what he was talking about. Each lesson actually lasted two or three months, he said. Only four or five messages a year! The result? A changed church. Communication had been established between God and His people. They became doers of the Word and not hearers only. They became—good soil.

31

Here, then, is what it takes to be good soil for the Word of God:

concentration on the Speaker and His Word,
commitment to the relationship between you and your Lord,
application of the Word in your practical daily life.

Be good soil.

NOTES

[1]Dwight L. Moody, *The Way to God* (Chicago: Revell, 1884), p. 7

[2]*Mr. William Shakespeare's Comedies, Histories & Tragedies,* ed. John Heminge and Henrie Condell (London: Printed by Isaac Jaggard and Ed Blount, 1623).

[3]New York: Association Press, 1923, p. 11.

[4]*The Modern Tradition,* ed. Richard Ellman and Charles Feidelson, Jr. (New York: Oxford University Press, 1965), p. 189.

IV. PRAY THEN LIKE THIS

Luke 18:1-14

These two parables don't teach all we need to know about prayer, but what they teach is very important. Both stories are about God; more specifically, they are about what God expects of us when we pray.

He expects us to be persistent, and He insists that we approach Him with humility.

PERSISTENCE IN PRAYER

"Then Jesus told his disciples a parable to show them that they should always pray and not give up" (Luke 18:1). He is not comparing God to the unjust judge, of course. Just the opposite. His point is that even such a scoundrel as this unscrupulous judge will give the woman what she wants, if only to have done with her pestering.

When Jesus speaks of widows, we pay attention. He notes a poor widow's sacrificial offering at the temple (Mark 12:41-44), He scolds religious leaders for taking advantage of helpless widows (Mark 12:40), and He makes certain that his own mother will be cared for after His death (John 19:26, 27). Always the champion of the downtrodden, Jesus takes the side of persons who cannot defend themselves. A woman without a husband was a pitiful person in Jesus' day. Dependent upon others, having almost no legal rights, a widow would have no clout with a judge. He could ignore her plight with impunity. Her situation would be desperate. She could not bargain; she could only beg for justice.

So this widow begs, repeatedly. Her problem must be money, since she brings her case to a single judge and not an assembled tribunal, which would be the case otherwise. Her condition is complicated by her poverty. She is too poor to bribe the judge, and the system seldom works without oiling the palms of the greedy officials. All she has on her side is stubborn determination to get what is coming to her. She hounds the judge until he can't stand the sight of her. He yields in order to buy some peace.

Jesus' little story makes three statements about prayer:

1) *Pray always.* Reduced to the language of the street, the moral of the story is the familiar axiom, "The squeaking axle gets the grease." In loftier language, it sounds like a Psalm:

"But I call to God,
 and the Lord saves me.
Evening, morning and noon
 I cry out in distress,
 and he hears my voice" (Psalm 55:16, 17).

The apostle Paul picked up the same theme in Ephesians 6:18:

"Pray in the Spirit on all occasions with all kinds of prayers and requests. With this in mind, be alert and always *keep on praying* for all the saints."

And again in 1 Thessalonians 5:16-18:

"Be joyful always; pray continually; give thanks in all circumstances. . . ."

Don't stop praying. Don't worry that you will offend God by your unceasing petitions, for you won't. "Will not God bring about justice for his chosen ones, who cry out to him day and night? Will he keep putting them off?" (Luke 18:7).

2) *Don't lose heart.* It may not appear for the moment that God is hearing and responding, but God will bring about justice for His chosen ones. There is nothing final about your current circumstances. God hasn't said the last word yet. You may be tempted to become discouraged with nothing going right. With trouble behind and trouble around and trouble ahead, you may feel like echoing Disraeli's famous lament, "Youth is a blunder, manhood a struggle, old age a regret." Nothing seems right at any age. But don't lose heart. God does not ignore the pleas of his petitioners. He still has your best interests at heart and will "give good gifts to those who ask him" (Matthew 7:11). In everything "God works for the good of those who love him, who have been called according to his purpose" (Romans 8:28). So don't give up.

3) *And don't worry about the final outcome.* You can trust Him. He is just the opposite of this corrupt judge. He is just, He is merciful, and He is faithful to keep His promises. You can relax and enjoy His providential care. You can be at peace. Matthew Henry's famous Bible commentary explains the Christian's unnatural peace of mind. He says that when Christ was about to leave the world, He made His will. He committed His soul to His Father, He bequeathed His body to Joseph of Arimathea, His

34

clothes fell to the soldiers, He entrusted the care of His mother to John. "But what should He leave to His poor disciples, that had left all for Him? Silver and gold had He none; but He left them that which was infinitely better, His peace. 'Peace I leave with you, my peace I give to you.' "

In that plan we live, confident that God will hear and respond to our persistent prayers.

Something Jesus doesn't say about praying in this manner, which should be mentioned here, is the effect such steadfastness has on the pray-er. If it finally moves God as the widow's petitions compel the crooked judge to decide justly, this kind of prayer does even more to the one praying. It changes His life. Habitual prayer shapes character. It brightens personality, it warms the heart, it engenders hope. You cannot pray with persistence and remain unchanged.

The famed American psychologist William James laid down three maxims for making "our nervous system our ally instead of our enemy." He insists that "we must make automatic and habitual, as early as possible, as many useful actions as we can." To do so, we should

1) "Launch ourselves with as strong and decisive an initiative as possible." He means that you should start the project determined to bring it to a successful conclusion. Be committed!

2) "Never suffer an exception to occur till the new habit is securely rooted in your life." Be consistent, unwavering— persistent!

3) "Seize the very first possible opportunity to act on every resolution you make, and on every emotional prompting you may experience in the direction of the habits you aspire to gain."[1]

Pray morning and evening, in public and private, on schedule and on impulse. Only by acting, and acting in spite of the cost to yourself, can you change your character. But if you follow these principles, you will change.

Most people would agree that "prayer changes things." Prayer also changes pray-ers. The secret is persistence.

While attending a national convocation of Christian leaders at Stanford University a few years ago, I was inspired when the dean of the chapel there, Dr. Robert Hamerton-Kelley, led us in repeating a fifteenth century prayer:

35

"God be in my heart and in my understanding.
God be in mine eyes and in my looking.
God be in my mouth and in my speaking.
God be in my heart and in my thinking.
God be at mine end and at my departing."

This is what Jesus is talking about, prayer that does not give up, prayer that dominates your very being, prayer that immerses you in the thoughts of God. Persistent prayer.

HUMILITY IN PRAYER

Such persistence as we have been talking about is a natural outgrowth of humility. It recognizes that God is everything, that apart from Him we are nothing. It concentrates the attention on God and forgets self. "Prayer," as Simone Weil has written,

"consists of attention. It is the orientation of all the attention of which the soul is capable toward God. The quality of the attention counts for much in the quality of the prayer. Warmth of heart cannot make up for it."[2]

To concentrate on God like this will drive out from the heart any impulse to boast. "Woe is me," Isaiah cried when he came into the presence of God. "I am ruined! For I am a man of unclean lips, and I live among a people of unclean lips, and my eyes have seen the King, the Lord Almighty!" (Isaiah 6:5). To stand before the Holy God, to gaze upon His purity, forces your eyes downward, compels a beating of breast and a murmuring, "God, have mercy on me, a sinner" (Luke 18:13).

Humility is self-forgetfulness. Like the widow who forgets about herself—her reputation, the danger she could be in, the consequences if she infuriates the judge—the tax collector in Jesus' story finds nothing to boast of in himself. He is in the presence of God.

The Pharisee, on the other hand, seems almost unaware that God exists, or if He does, He is little more than a divine eavesdropper on this conversation between the man and his favorite audience, himself. "The Pharisee stood up and prayed *about* himself" (Luke 18:11). A footnote to that verse adds that he could be praying *to* himself. Whichever preposition you choose, the tone is the same. The man embodies the self-righteousness that Jesus cannot abide. He prohibits His disciples from imitating this man's style. Such prayers are hypocrisy, and such pray-ers are only play-actors. "But when you pray, do not be like the hypo-

36

crites, for they love to pray standing in the synagogues and on the street corners to be seen by men" (Matthew 6:5). They will get what they want: they will be seen by men, and that's the end of the matter. "They have their reward." Their conversation is not with God.

In this, as in so many other matters, we would do well to learn from a child, one little lad in particular. He was saying his go-to-bed prayers in a very low voice.

"I can't hear you, dear," his mother whispered.

"I wasn't talking to you," he told her. His prayer was for God!

A prayer to God humbles the petitioner. It does not demand of God, but prepares to do God's bidding. At the end of Tennessee William's play, *The Milk Train Doesn't Stop Here Anymore*, a dying Flora cries out in an anguished voice, "Bring God to me! . . . How do you do it, whistle, ring a bell for him?" She rings her little dinner bell three times, but God does not come running.

That's not God's way. He never comes when He is rung for like a divine bell-hop. He will always be God, in spite of our plots to usurp His throne and make *Him* serve *us*. "Hallowed be your name," Jesus taught us to pray. Only He is God. We are His dependents; He is not ours. "Seek the Lord while he may be found; call on him while he is near" (Isaiah 55:6). The prophets never forget the freedom of God. He can withdraw if He desires. He stoops in love to save us, but never in fear to obey us.

George Müller of Bristol, England, is one of Christian history's best illustrators of the power of humble praying. When he began rescuing Bristol's orphans in what grew to become an enormous mission, he established the rule for the orphanage to be the same as the rule of his life: he would never ask for money, even to save lives, of anyone except the Lord. He would trust God to provide everything he and the children needed. He would not promote, publicize his needs, or in any way compromise his posture of total dependence upon God.

Several times his principle was sorely tested, but every time his persistent, humble prayers were sufficient. On one such occasion of severe financial distress, he received a letter from a Christian brother who had often given money to help Müller:

"Have you any *present* need for the Institution under your care? I know you do not *ask*, except indeed of Him whose work you are doing; but to *answer when asked* seems another thing, and a right thing. I have reason for desiring to know the present state of your means toward the objects you are labouring to serve: viz., should you *not have* need, other departments of the Lord's work, or other people of the Lord, *may have* need. Kindly then inform me, and to what amount, i.e., what amount you at this present time need or can profitably lay out."

The request seems very reasonable to me. But not to Müller. He had staked everything on his great experiment, which was to prove that prayer to God alone would solve every crisis. When Müller received this friend's letter, he had only twenty-seven pence ha'penny in all, a pittance, to feed hundreds of orphans. In spite of his distress, he replied,

"Whilst I thank you for your love, and whilst I agree with you that, in general, there is a difference between *asking for money* and *answering when asked,* nevertheless, in our case, I feel not at liberty to speak about the state of our funds, as the primary object of the work in my hands is to lead those who are weak in faith to see that there is *reality* in dealing with God alone."[3]

His concentration on God and God's ability was total. His humility before God's ability was absolute.

By the way, the inquiring Christian brother, who could get no statement of need from Müller, sent him one hundred pounds—which arrived when not a penny was left.

Müller was not afraid to ask God. He had the faith of the widow before her judge and the humble concentration on God of the penitent tax collector. He did not enter into prayer lightly, nor did he take on his gargantuan task of rescuing children without counting the cost. His confidence was in knowing that what he was unable to do for God, God could do for him and the children.

There is something childlike about a man like Müller or like Jesus' tax collector. The sinner who confesses his sin and the benefactor who looks only to God for support exhibit the trustfulness of a child. They had not made up their minds about what is possible and impossible, what God can and will do and what He can not and will not do.

If there is something they want, they ask for it; they do not stand on their dignity or feel ashamed to bow before the Lord. When their Father says, "Trust me," they trust Him. When He tells them to ask, seek, and knock, that is exactly what they do.

It is fair to say, I suppose, that prayer, which is so baffling to the worldly wise, is really for the child. The wise man relies on his wisdom, the proud man on his pride, the rich man on his wealth, the powerful man on his power, the religious man on his religiousness. But the child—or the adult who has turned and become like a child (Luke 18:17)—does not expect God to be his servant. He makes himself God's child, and like a child, tells the Father of his needs, desires, sins, and sorrows. Prayer is not a ritual; it is at the heart of his life experience. It expresses his true self. His attention is on the source of his life, and when he is in touch with his source, he is at his best.

NOTES

[1]*The Principles of Psychology* (Henry Holt and Co., 1890), pp. 120ff.
[2]*The Simone Weil Reader,* George A. Panichas, ed. (New York: David McKay Company, 1977), p. 44.
[3]A. T. Pierson, *George Müller of Bristol* (Old Tappan: Revell), pp. 166, 167.

V. WHAT REAL CHRISTIANS LOOK LIKE

Matthew 7:15-27

What is virtue?

Socrates, leading philosopher of ancient Athens, the world's most famous debating society, believed that "daily to discourse about virtue . . . is the greatest good of man." From Socrates to the present, scholars have fine-tuned their definitions of this supreme excellence, calling it, among other things, "moral and mental achievement of the highest order." To the Greeks, it meant academic or mental greatness, a definition that fostered Greece's love of debate and disdain of physical work. Jesus would have squirmed through those debates. To Him, virtue could never be achieved through mental gymnastics. Virtue is not something you think, but something you actually do.

The way of life Jesus teaches is an energetic one. It consists of bearing fruit and doing God's will. It means hearing Jesus' Word and doing it. Real Christians look like doers of the Word, and not hearers only.

REAL CHRISTIANS BEAR GOOD FRUIT

Jesus warns against false prophets—phonies who dress like prophets, sound like prophets, trick innocents into following them as prophets, but who poison their devotees with bad fruit.

It is a good warning for these closing days of the twentieth century, when prophets called futurologists are getting rich outguessing tomorrow. Futurology is a flourishing industry today. Optimists predict a coming utopia, and pessimists forecast another world war, followed by a collapse of human civilization into a society of savages.

You can take your pick of prophets. If you believe in the reign of the stars, there are astrologers aplenty to read your horoscope. If you are of a Marxist turn of mind, convinced that man is basically a product of the economy, you will have no trouble finding economists to accommodate you. Strange that anyone should trust an economist after our national experience with these experts, but they keep making the headlines in spite of their record. There are political pundits and every shade of business consultant and even the mystic utterances of Indian gurus at your service, for a fee, of course. I haven't mentioned the scientific and pseudo-scientific seers in such diverse fields as biogenetics and social anthropology and inorganic chemistry and physics, a smorgasbord of selections to satisfy any inquisitive temperament.

I must not leave out those religious prophets hawking their wares over radio and television airwaves, most of them announcing the imminent end of the world when the Lord returns on such and such a day. As I write these words in Arizona, one of our local celebrities has just missed another date for the Lord's return. Not to worry, he has quickly recalculated and, admitting a slight mathematical error for the umpteenth time, he is now certain he has found Christ's real and final arrival time.

The future tantalizes us all, of course, like some forbidden fruit that we'll dine with the devil to taste. It has always been so. Even Jesus' disciples were easy prey, so Jesus had to caution them against their gullibility:

"At that time if anyone says to you, 'Look, here is the Christ!' or, 'There he is!' do not believe it. For false Christs and false prophets will appear and perform great signs and miracles to deceive even the elect—if that were possible. See, I have told you ahead of time" (Matthew 24:23-25).

His warning was echoed by the leaders of the struggling new Christian church. In writing to the troubled Corinthian congregation, the apostle Paul speaks of "false apostles, deceitful workmen, masquerading as apostles of Christ. And no wonder, for Satan himself masquerades as an angel of light" (2 Corinthians 11:13, 14). When Paul takes leave of the elders of the Ephesian church, he cautions them about certain trouble ahead:

"I know that after I leave, savage wolves will come in among you and will not spare the flock. Even from your own number men will arise and distort the truth in order to draw away disciples after them" (Acts 20:29).

John gently writes in a similar vein:

"Dear friends, do not believe every spirit, but test the spirits to see whether they are from God, because many false prophets have gone out into the world" (1 John 4:1).

They have indeed!

Prophet has two meanings. It refers basically to one who acts as a spokesman for God. He is a truth-teller. If he tells the truth about his day, however, with his inspired insight into meanings and consequences, he naturally traces those consequences into the future. In his truth-telling, he then becomes a future-teller. Sometimes God even blesses him with a special disclosure of some future events, matters of which he could never have known apart from God's revelation. The true prophet, then, is a simple truth-sayer.

It is at once an enviable and a dreaded occupation. A roll call of the prophets invokes memories of the misery these men of God endured on behalf of the truth they spoke. Joseph languished in prison, John the Baptist was beheaded, Jeremiah suffered ridicule and physical anguish, and on and on goes the list. True prophets don't go into the future-foretelling business to make money or become famous or to enjoy the company of kings. Having received the word of the Lord, their cry is "Woe is me! I am ruined!" (Isaiah 6:5).

Yet, if you are not terribly concerned about things like justice and righteousness and truth, the life of the prophet is not so bad after all. There is certainly no lack of an audience. The weak gladly follow authoritarian personalities, the mentally lazy are pleased to have someone else do their thinking for them, and the morally obtuse prefer that someone else spell out what's right and wrong. Unfortunately, most people are afraid, so when someone looks and sounds like—and claims to be—a prophet, they obediently follow.

False utterances can have a ring of truth about them, at least to the undiscerning. False teachers will tell you that what you have heard from others about Jesus being God in the flesh is not really true (1 John 4:2, 3). That sounds good, since the incarnation is a difficult doctrine to comprehend, anyway. They will forbid marriage and order abstinence from eating certain foods, and they will certainly require you to forego sex as well (1 Timothy 4:1f). False prophets major in the religious "Thou shalt not"; they glory in secret rites and sacrifices; they present themselves as father figures before frightened children; they guarantee their followers ease or success or an escape from the pressures of competitive society. They are, for the most part, impressive authority figures.

Too bad they are phonies. You can judge them by their fruits. Given time enough and rope, they will hang themselves—or you. They feed themselves but not the poor. They clothe themselves but not the naked. They visit their friends but not the imprisoned. They preach peace when there is no peace and counsel wisdom when they are themselves unwise. They build their mansions from sacrificial offerings of hovel dwellers; they call for sacrifice so they can be more comfortable. They bear no fruit worthy of repentance; they do no work expressive of Christian faith; they love only themselves.

They look like sheep, but they devour.

They are not real Christians; they bear no good fruit.

REAL CHRISTIANS DO THE WILL OF GOD

Talking isn't enough. Prophesying isn't enough. Jesus does not deny that religious phonies can sometimes perform miracles or drive out demons or even utter prophecies in His name. But because they call on the Lord does not mean that the Lord has called or authorized them. In this regard, He agrees with James, "Be ye doers of the word and not hearers only, deceiving your own selves," as the King James Version translates James 1:22. The New International Version is stronger: "Do not merely listen to the word, and so deceive yourselves. *Do what it says.*"

It takes no conviction to say, "Lord, Lord," but to bend a stubborn will to the Father is something else.

Jesus values obedience. In Matthew 21:28-32, His story of two brothers is recorded. Their father said to the first one, "Son, go and work today in the vineyard."

"I will not," the son answered, but later he changed his mind and did what his father asked him.

To the second son the father made the same request. "I will, sir," the young man respectfully replied. But he did not go.

"Which of the two *did* what his father wanted?" Jesus asked His audience. Then, lest they should miss His point, He added, "I tell you the truth, the tax collectors and the prostitutes are entering the kingdom of God ahead of you." He was speaking to religious types who were accustomed to intoning, "Lord, Lord," but failing to repent when He asked for repentance and to obey when He asked for obedience. In spite of all their protestations of loyalty, they have no right to expect the Lord to count them among His own.

Jesus was speaking as Savior, sent to a troubled world. He knew only God could save humanity, and only an obedient humanity could be rescued. Words and random motions weren't good enough.

44

Europe was in trouble in 1938 when President Roosevelt convened a conference at Evian-Les-Bains, France. World leaders assembled to devise solutions to the peril of the Jews in Hitler's Germany and in the recently invaded Austria. It was an historic meeting, for the conference had a chance to affect the course of modern civilization and save the desperate foes of the Nazis. It failed. Completely. Six million Jews died because of its failure.

An old man, the concierge at the Royal Hotel in those days, recently reminisced about the conference. He recalled all the quite important people having a grand time together. They took pleasure cruises on the lake, gambled every night in the casino, bathed in the mineral waters, and yielded their recreation-weary bodies to France's finest masseurs. Not to be overlooked were the excursions to Chamonix to do a little summer skiing and the horseback rides on the fine steeds from the best stables in France. Oh, they also golfed.[1]

Some even attended the meetings. But if they were a little lax, how can you blame them, with all the seductions of this famed resort beckoning?

So they wined and dined and played and laughed and sent in reports to their various governments, assuring the folks back home that everything was quite good and they did intend to do something about Hitler and the doomed Jews. "Yes sir," they said, "we'll get right on it." But they did not.

"Many will say to me on that day, 'Lord, Lord. . . .' "

What Jesus wants is action.

REAL CHRISTIANS PRACTICE WHAT JESUS PREACHES

The wise man "hears these words of mine and puts them into practice" (Matthew 7:24). He listens, and he hears, and he *does*. In the Sermon on the Mount, Jesus calls for action. As Dr. L. P. Jacks has written, "Every truth that religion announces passes instantly into a command. Its indicatives are veiled imperatives."

"I myself must mix with action," Tennyson exclaimed, "lest I wither by despair." There is no alternative. Without putting Jesus' words into practice, you will never know their truth and receive His blessings. When the rains fall, so will you.

A recent *Peanuts* strip shows Charlie Brown and a little friend talking. Actually, she's talking and he's just listening. She tells him about her uncle who has always wanted to play the violin.

45

Finally, last week, he went to a music store and bought himself one. Then he went to a concert so he could watch the violinists play to see how they did it. Then he went home, picked up his new violin and tried to play it. But he couldn't, not at all! "So," she tells Charlie Brown, "the next time he goes to a concert, he's going to try sitting closer!"

He'll never learn to play.

He's like some Christians who have decided they want to become better disciples of Jesus. They go to church services Sunday morning, and then they return on Sunday evening, and then they take in a midweek service. They watch the preacher preach and they watch the teacher teach. But they never learn how to play. They hear. They say, "Lord, Lord." But they do not put Jesus' words into practice.

As a pastor, I am painfully aware of our members' problems. Many are anxious, tense, frustrated, and even ill. What hurts is that they could be cured, if they would. They do not need more therapy or longterm counseling or more attention to themselves. Especially they don't need to pay any more attention to themselves! They just need to practice what Jesus preaches. They need to build their lives on the sure foundation of His truth.

What He has taught is eternal wisdom. To heed Him is to live; to reject His counsel is to invite illness and death.

On a miserable January afternoon in 1982, Air Florida Flight #90 was waiting for clearance to take off. Twice the plane had been de-iced according to FAA regulations, and the co-pilot noticed that the wings were icing up badly again. "Boy, this is a losing battle trying to de-ice those things." He wasn't convinced the procedure did much good anyway. "It [gives] you a false sense of security, that's all it does." His pilot agreed that it "satisfied the Feds," but did not seem alarmed that the idle plane was accumulating more and more of the weighty ice. So they did not de-ice a third time.

This brief conversation is now famous. It is available on tape. It was fished out of the river into which the plane plunged after hitting a Washington bridge on its attempted takeoff. As the plane raced down the runway the pilots knew they were in trouble. The co-pilot asked his superior, "Do you want me to do anything special for it or just go for it?" They went for it, but the ice the pilots had decided to ignore cost their lives and those of 72 other people on board. Four motorists who just happened to

46

be driving across the bridge at the wrong moment also died.[2]

The pilots didn't mean to kill the passengers. They didn't think it was a serious offense to ignore the ruling to de-ice their plane. They meant well. They just did not do what they were told. And when the storm rose, they fell.

Like a house built on sand.

NOTES

[1] Joseph Bayly, "Out of My Mind," *Eternity* (August, 1978), p. 41.
[2] "We're Going Down, Larry," *Time* (February 15, 1982), p. 21.

VI. IS GOD ALWAYS FAIR?

Matthew 20:1-16

Is God always fair? No, not always. Sometimes He is more than fair. When He strikes a bargain with His people, He always keeps His side of it—and then goes beyond—even if He appears to some people to be unfair.

What angered the Pharisees and other religious leaders about Jesus' teaching was His disregard for their doctrine of God's justice. He seemed to be telling people that the very religious among them, who worked so hard to observe every little jot and tittle of the law in order to please God, would get no more from God than people who did little or nothing for Him. Furthermore, Jesus also was claiming that the Jews, God's very own people, would have to share God's blessing with Gentiles. "That's not fair!" they protested.

"The Workers in the Vineyard" is Jesus' answer to His critics. Agreeing with them that from their point of view God does not govern with strict justice, He hopes to show them that there is something better than "fairness." Look carefully at what Jesus teaches about God's call to work, His standard of justice, and His generosity. Then contrast these virtues with the workers' selfishness.

GOD'S CALL TO WORK

The parable is not about work, of course, but our country's growing disdain of labor causes me to pause for a moment on this aspect of the story. Work does not carry the stigma in the Scriptures that today's pleasure-seekers have ascribed to it. Sometimes the kingdom of God is compared to a party (see Luke 14:16-24), a happy simile that stresses the celebrating and gaiety that are to be eternally enjoyed in the presence of the Lord. In this parable, however, Jesus likens the kingdom to working in a vineyard. Our understanding of the kingdom requires both comparisons, because we have already learned that there can be no genuine joy in life apart from meaningful work. Neither can there be any real faith unless that faith is expressed in action: "Faith by itself, if it is not accompanied by action, is dead. . . . Show me

49

your faith without deeds, and I will show you my faith by what I do" (James 2:17, 18).

In comparing God's kingdom with working, Jesus sounds like a good Jew. If anything distinguished ancient Israel from the other great civilization from which Western culture descends, ancient Greece, it was Judaism's firm conviction that there is dignity in physical labor. The glory of Greece—the Parthenon, for example—was constructed by great gangs of laborers whose achievements with rollers and levers and incredible physical exertion are a wonder to modern man. But their compatriots had little praise for them. The Greeks marveled over the beauty of the Parthenon and their other architectural monuments but, if we can trust the documents that survive from that pre-Christian era, they neither admired nor respected the laborers who built them. They were mere instruments, like modern machines and tools, to be used and discarded when used up. Even the enlightened Plato relegated craftsmen to the lowest rungs of the social ladder. Aristotle, going Plato one better, sniffed that "the best ordered state will not make an artisan a citizen." He was *just* a laborer.

We praise Athens for its great philosophers, but we must turn to Israel to learn that God values every human being, including manual laborers. In Israel, everybody worked. Even God (Genesis 2:2; John 5:17). The whole nation was regarded as a workfield (Isaiah 5:1-7). The Son of God was a carpenter, and His disciples were called builders, farmhands, and fishermen. Paul's inspired instructions to the Thessalonians are in this tradition:

"Make it your ambition to lead a quiet life, to mind your own business and to work with your hands, just as we told you, so that your daily life may win the respect of outsiders and so that you will not be dependent on anybody" (1 Thessalonians 4:11, 12).

Earlier I mentioned America's growing disdain of work. I am not exaggerating. I read that in 1980, the average non-agricultural worker in the United States worked 35 hours and 36 minutes a week. *Time* concludes, "Because of that effort, America can now claim title to a dubious superlative: world's shortest work week."[1] Do you suppose there is any correlation between this new record and America's slipping ability to compete in the world's marketplace?

It's more than possible that this general disregard for honest hard work has poisoned Christian attitudes as well. If this is not so, why do we think of ministers, doctors, and professors as being "called" to their vocations, but we never use this term when referring to janitors, plumbers, or carpenters? A re-study of 1 Thessalonians 4:11, 12; 2 Thessalonians 3:11-13; and Romans 12:3-13 will help us regain God's perspective on work. Then we'll sing with more integrity, "My Master was a worker, with daily work to do, And he who would be like him must be a worker too. . . ."[2]

GOD'S JUSTICE

The central issue in this parable is God's justice. Is it fair that those who work only one hour should receive the same wage as those who labor all day? It certainly isn't, if we are thinking in hours. But if our real concern is keeping men and their families from starving, and if it takes practically all of a day's wage to buy enough food to feed a family for one day, is it "fair" to pay for only one hour? Does a man have a "right" to live? Does the Master have a "right" to deprive him of life if he has the resources to keep the man from starving?

The question of justice is not an easy one. For as long as man has thought about God, he has questioned His justice. So many things in this world seem unfair. Yet, as Dorothy Sayers has written,

"When we demand justice, it is always justice on our behalf against other people. Nobody, I imagine, would ever ask for justice to be done upon him for everything he ever did wrong. We do not want justice—we want revenge: and that is why, when justice is done upon us, we cry out that God is vindictive."[3]

So Thomas Jefferson, contemplating the white man's cruelty to Negro slaves, had reason to worry: "I tremble for my country when I remember that God is just!" Abraham Lincoln later quoted Jefferson, with whom he differed widely in theology but shared a conviction that God would one day judge the works of men. Lincoln feared God's justice as much as Jefferson did.

So did Shakespeare. When his Polonius tells Hamlet that he would treat some fellows "according to their desert," Hamlet rebukes him:

"God's bodykins, man, much better. Use every man after his desert, and who should escape whipping? Use them after your

51

own honour and dignity; the less they deserve the more merit is in your bounty."[4]

Since we all deserve the whipping, do we really want justice?

What *kind* of justice do we want? During America's great depression, among the hardest hit were the farmers (then one-quarter of our population). A bushel of wheat that sold in Chicago for $2.94 in 1920 went for one dollar by 1929 and 30 cents by 1932. Farmers were desperate. They demanded justice. When Judge Charles Bradley foreclosed on a series of mortgages—in the name of justice—a crowd of maddened farmers kidnapped him from his courtroom, drove him out into the countryside and began to lynch him. When he was nearly unconscious they let him drop, placed a truck hubcap on his head and forced him to his knees. His prayer? "O Lord, I pray thee, do justice to all men."[5]

Whose justice did he want? For himself? For them? For their mortgagors?

Let's ask the question again, if only to strengthen our case for questioning the human demand for justice. Most Americans love to boast of their Civil War as a great victory for justice. The freeing of the slaves fulfilled the promise of the Declaration of Independence for all Americans, even those who had been shackled. Surely all men should rejoice that justice had been achieved. Yet when Lincoln issued his famous Emancipation Proclamation, now considered one of his greatest achievements, he was broadly condemned. A leading British journal charged that this "monstrous, reckless, devilish" proclamation aligned Lincoln with Beelzebub himself. The journal attributed the North's pursuit of the war to nothing but greed. The Emancipation Proclamation justified the South's rebellion, this writer complained.

When I first ran across such statements, I could hardly believe my eyes. How could anybody fail to see the justice of setting the slaves free? How could the journal attack the North's position as economically motivated? How could it justify the slaveholders?

But there is some truth in the charges. Certainly it was unjust that hundreds of thousands of innocent men should die for something that was not their fault. Further, it *was* unfair that thousands of farms were destroyed, that more thousands of families were left without husbands and fathers. And how should we account for the fact that Christians in the South prayed just as fervently as

Christians in the North, yet Southern prayers apparently were denied?

Is it really justice that we want, or something more?

I have raised my own whimiscal complaints regarding an injustice I have had to live with. Why, Oh Lord, couldn't you have made me tall? Or at least average? Why short? I have not been entirely serious, especially in my more mature years. I have come to realize the many advantages of being short—cheaper maintenance costs, more comfort in airplane seats, a choice of buying clothes in the men's department or the boys', fewer bumps on the head, and a lot of laughter. But it does not seem altogether fair, just the same, that I should do all the looking up to others.

My friend Chuck Boatman, after suffering through a speech in which I must have told one too many short jokes, presented me with this limerick, tastefully penned on the back of his table placemat:

There once was a Lawson from Mesa
Who took up not very much space-a.
   Although he was short,
   He would quickly retort:
"I am what I am by God's grace-a."

GOD'S GENEROSITY

Now we have come to the essence of Jesus' story. God's grace, His generosity, explains the Master's treatment of all His workers. He is thinking of the workmen's needs. If they go home with wages for only a single hour, or three hours, they will not have enough to feed their families. The eleventh hour recruit needed work as much as the first ones selected. He would not have waited all day in the marketplace otherwise. The law provided that a worker should be paid the day's wages at the end of each day (Leviticus 19:13; Deuteronomy 24:15). Most workers lived a hand-to-mouth existence. There was nothing to fall back on. No savings accounts, no unemployment compensation, no food stamps. Nothing. The employer's concern was that each worker should have enough for food for the day; to pay less would have been, from his point of view, unfair.

What seems unfair to the selfish workers may really have been unjust, when weighed from the hourly-wage point of view. But to demand strict justice could be nothing less than unmerciful, and the employer seeks to be merciful. He does not dismiss them with a calloused wave of the hand and an unthinking, "They are without food because they are mere idlers. They couldn't find work; that's their trouble."

What characterizes this master is his ability to see things from someone else's point of view. When he does so, he immediately grasps their real need and treats it. A famous professor of an earlier generation has recounted the day he went into a crowded railroad dining car for lunch. It was a sweltering day, so when the steward handed him his menu, he remarked that the cooks in the kitchen must be suffering. The steward was surprised. He told the professor that he was accustomed to people coming in complaining about the food, the service, and the heat, but that in his nineteen years of service, he was the first person who ever expressed any sympathy for the cooks in the kitchen.

No one had ever thought to adopt the cooks' point of view. This is what makes the master in Jesus' story so remarkable: he looks upon every worker as a human being with needs, and he determines to meet those needs regardless of the legalist's criticism. He gives according to needs, not according to the strict calculations of the company pursor. His generosity overrules his business sense. He embodies Jesus' teaching elsewhere:

"The King will reply, 'I tell you the truth, whatever you did for one of the least of these brothers of mine, you did for me' " (Matthew 25:40).

"Go back and report to John what you hear and see: The blind receive sight, the lame walk, those who have leprosy are cured, the deaf hear, the dead are raised, and the good news is preached to the poor" (Matthew 11:4, 5).

Jesus was echoing the concern of the prophets:

"Strengthen the feeble hands,
    steady the knees that give way;
say to those with fearful hearts,
    'Be strong, do not fear;
your God will come,
    he will come with vengeance;
with divine retribution
    he will come to save you.'
Then will the lame leap like a deer,
    and the tongue of the dumb shout for joy" (Isaiah 35:3-6).

Scripture offers grace, not justice. The word *grace* does not appear often in the Gospels—only in Luke and in John's prologue. *Mercy* as a noun is also missing. But the meaning is there. It is there in this employer's overpayment of his workers; it is there in the father's joyous reception of his prodigal son; it is there in Jesus' forgiveness of the woman taken in adultery, in His healings on the Sabbath, in His acceptance of the unacceptable, in His refusal to condemn persons because of their past sins, in His free gift of a new chance in life, and in His ready welcome of prostitutes and tax collectors into His circle of friends.

Grace becomes a more frequent word in Acts and the epistles, because it characterizes the life of the early church. The concordance shows that *grace* is used only fifteen times in the Bible up to the book of Acts, but from then on it appears at least one hundred times. Paul never tires of rejoicing, as he writes to the Romans, that in Christ "we have gained access by faith into this grace in which we now stand" (5:2). The church at Rome was, like the others, filled with humble, frail, often disappointing men and women. Only grace allowed them into the church, and only grace—God's grace to them and their grace with each other—could keep them there. From God's generosity, we learn the generosity without which no human bonds can hold.

THE WORKERS' SELFISHNESS

I wish this part of the story did not have to be told. The employer's generosity is under attack. This is Jesus' reason for telling the story. He has answered God's critics. They have resented the whole truth of His ministry, His reckless embracing of those who did not "deserve" God's favor. The workers' grumbling against their generous employer is no uglier than the critics' carping, their hateful, merciless attempt to exclude all but themselves from God's embrace.

I do not wish to dwell on these men. Let me borrow the following story from another preacher and be done with it.

"The devil was once crossing the Libyan Desert when he came upon a group of small fiends who were tempting a holy hermit. They tried him with the seductions of the flesh: they sought to sow his mind with doubts and fears: they told him that all his austerities were nothing worth. But it was all of no avail. The holy man was impeccable. Then the devil stepped forward. Addressing the imps he said: 'Your methods are too crude. Permit me for one moment. This is what I should recommend.' Going up to the hermit, he said: 'Have you heard the news? Your brother has been made Bishop of Alexandria.' The fable says, 'A scowl of malignant jealousy clouded the serene face of the holy man.' "[6]

Could it be that beneath our self-righteous demands for justice lies the real motive—jealousy?

But is that fair?

NOTES

[1]February 2, 1981.

[2]Words by William G. Tarrant.

[3]*Introductory Papers on Dante* (New York: Harper and Brothers, 1954), p. 67.

[4]*Hamlet,* II, ii, p. 552.

[5]*Time,* February 1, 1982, p. 30.

[6]Quoted by W. E. Sangster, *The Craft of the Sermon* (Philadelphia: The Westminster Press, 1951), p. 32.

VII. ON NOT REMAINING IMMATURE INDEFINITELY

Matthew 13:31-33

When time is fleeting, you have to grow up in a hurry. In a *Peanuts* strip, Charlie Brown's dog, Snoopy, is thinking over a conversation he just had with a fruitfly. "He told me he had only one regret," Snoopy tells Woodstock after learning that some fruitflies live only twenty-four hours. "He said, 'I wish I knew at nine o'clock what I know now.' "[1] You have to learn fast when all you have is a day.

Unfortunately, when you have three score and ten years to live, growing up doesn't seem so important. Some people seem never to mature. It is as if their watches stopped at a certain hour and they've never moved past it. Their bodies age, but their behavior remains childish.

The famous German poet, Goethe, observed that "everybody wants to *be* somebody: nobody wants to grow." His judgment is too harsh, although he is more guilty of exaggerating than of lying. It does seem that for the majority of mankind the eagerness of the child to mature has been replaced by the fear of the adult to change. Their arrested development has been captured in a delightful saying I ran across a few years ago. I liked it so much I have adopted it as my personal philosophy: "You can't help growing old, but you can remain immature indefinitely." I quote this wisdom often, especially after managing to embarrass myself yet again with another demonstration of my immaturity. It is always good for a laugh. But if my friends thought I really meant it, they would mourn for me rather than laugh. Perpetual immaturity is not funny. It is, unfortunately, rather widespread. It isn't easy to grow up, so many people choose not to.

"If only I may grow: firmer, simpler—quieter, warmer."[2] In this as in so many of his *Markings,* former United Nations General Secretary Dag Hammarskjold expresses the wish of thoughtful persons everywhere. We would like to blossom into a maturity marked by firmness, simplicity, quietness, and warmth. We really would. If only wishing could make it so.

A review of our lives reveals some things we like, but more that we regret. There hasn't been enough progress. Our characters seem insufficiently formed. What change or growth there is seems to have come about naturally, through no disciplined effort of our own. The movement from infancy through childhood and adolescence to adulthood just happened naturally. Then we stopped. Worse, the changes are no longer for the better. The body is decaying and the personality seems to be decaying with it. We must do something. The adult must *wish* to grow; more than that, he must *will* to grow, with a determination that cannot be daunted and a faith that overcomes fear of failure and fear of the future. When fear kills the will, growth is finished.

Jesus is speaking directly to this fear in these two little parables about the kingdom of Heaven. More than once His disciples must have protested against His dreams for them. They were realists. They could count. How could such a tiny handful of men stand up to the awesome power of Rome? So few and so weak, what could they do to right the wrongs of their world? They had heard all Jesus' promises about His kingdom, but so far they had seen scant proof that He was telling the truth. He had taken no stand against the Roman soldiers, nor had He made any move toward forging the necessary political alliances to establish His government. And what they had seen Him do had been far from comforting. They had watched the growing animosity of their Jewish leaders; they had shivered as He deliberately antagonized them with His bold proclamations. They still respected and wanted to follow Him, but He made them squirm, even protest, at His starkly radical demands.

They were also afraid of the crowds that surrounded them. Not all of Jesus' students were for real. Some were just curiosity seekers, drifting in and out of the circle. Others were genuine troublemakers, spoiling for a fight between Jesus and the authorities. Then there were always the freeloaders, hanging around for bits of truth and larger bits of bread. Early in his career, Jesus chose a dozen or so to be his prize pupils, his special disciples. He gave them concentrated attention, to be sure, but He also made himself far too accessible to these huge, clamoring crowds of men and women whose sincerity the disciples clearly doubted. They had not sacrificed everything to follow Jesus, as the twelve had.

The disciples could not keep their doubts from the Lord. To

calm their anxiety, He told them the parable of the sower, the seed, and the four types of soil. They must know that even at this early stage the kingdom of God is a mixture of the faithful and unfaithful, the sincere and the insincere. This is also the theme of His parable of the wheat and the weeds (Matthew 13:24-30).

His disciples—then and now—must not be deceived by the apparent weakness of His kingdom and the apparent might of secular powers. The kingdom may be tiny now, like a mustard seed, but it will not remain small. Yes, there may be few genuine disciples now, but they are as powerful as the tiny bit of yeast a woman uses to force a large batch of flour dough to rise. Mustard seed and yeast: two metaphors of growth and faith. Jesus is talking about not remaining immature indefinitely.

Listen to His first statement:

"HAVE FAITH IN THE KINGDOM. IT IS GROWING."

You seem to be just a handful of men. When you look around you, the kingdom seems miniscule, insignificant, almost invisible against the forces of evil in this world. If Jesus were speaking to twentieth-century disciples, He would say something like this: "Don't be fooled by your modern notion that only big is beautiful. Little can be beautiful, too."

Then He might quote His disciple Paul to us:

"God chose the weak things of the world to shame the strong. He chose the lowly things of this world and the despised things—and the things that are not—to nullify the things that are, so that no one may boast before him" (1 Corinthians 1:27-29).

He could also call on the prophet who named His birthplace: "But you, Bethlehem Ephrathah, though you are small among the clans of Judah, out of you will come for me one who will be ruler over Israel . . ." (Micah 5:2).

Don't despise yourself because you are few in number; don't despair of the kingdom because it is small now, like a mustard seed, for like that seed it will grow. It will not remain immature indefinitely.

I like William James' defense of small beginnings:

"As for me my bed is made: I am against bigness and greatness in all their forms, and with the invisible, molecular, moral forces that work from individual to individual, stealing in through the crannies of the world like so many soft rootlets, or like the capillary oozing of water, and yet rending the hardest monuments of man's pride, if you give them time. The bigger unit you deal with, the hollower, the more brutal, the more mendacious is the life displayed. So I am against all big organizations as such . . . and in favor of the eternal forces of truth which always work in the individual and immediately unsuccessful way, underdogs always until history comes, after they are long dead, and puts them on top."[3]

James urges the long view. What seems weak may be weak only for the moment. The mustard seed is deceptive. When it dies in fertile soil, the tiny object springs alive to a great size, like leaven in a lump of dough.

The kingdom will not remain immature, so have faith. It is growing already, but not by humanity's normal means. Its power is the dynamic of the Holy Spirit (Acts 1:8), by means of which the kingdom's citizens will do extraordinary things (Acts 4:7, 8). It is an irresistible force; no machinery or monuments of man's devising can render it immovable. Not always visible to the untrained eye, this force will insinuate itself into the very councils of the enemy and eat away the foundations of great empires. It will prove that big is not always beautiful.

The church has not always appreciated its real source of power. These parables came true, all right. The kingdom grew and grew, but as William James so acutely perceived, sometimes "the bigger unit you deal with, the hollower, the more brutal," and finally, the more beggarly the life of the organization. By the time the handful of original disciples had grown into the magnificent church of the Middle Ages, its pomp and splendor were the envy of the "civilized" world, but its heart was hollow. It had all the trappings of power, but the source was shut off. The church usurped the glory that was the Rome of the first century and banqueted on the empire's rottenness in the process. Big is not always beautiful.

What is beautiful about Jesus' kingdom is not its cathedrals, but its caring. Jesus anticipates the mature role of His disciples in His metaphor of the mustard seed. At first it is nothing, but when it grows into its fullness, the tiny unprotected seed becomes the protector, offering sanctuary to the birds of the air and shade to the creatures beneath its branches. Jesus is prophetic. Where the kingdom is at its best is in its protective service. What would this world have become without the churches, hospitals, schools, missions, and other ministries of the kingdom? Who else has done so much to feed the hungry, clothe the naked, liberate the imprisoned, elevate the downtrodden? Who else will?

What Jesus' disciples have to learn is that the kingdom does not grow for its own sake, but for the sake of the "birds that perch." That is why you must never lose faith in it, even when it appears insignificant. The kingdom will not be stilled. It will serve, even when hostile authorities try to stop it. Recent reports from Communist China, Communist Russia, and other totalitarian countries that have tried to kill off the kingdom are proof that the gates of Hell cannot prevail against it. By God's power it keeps serving, and by serving it grows. It dies only where it stops serving.

Have faith in the kingdom. It is growing.

Implied in Jesus' first statement is this second one:

"HAVE FAITH IN YOURSELF. YOU ARE GROWING, TOO."

Salt, light, and yeast. These are what Jesus wants His disciples to be. (See Matthew 5:13-16.) They are to be as indispensable as salt and light and as effervescent as yeast. There is no substitute for them. They are basic to life itself.

Many must have been the times that Jesus' first disciples wanted to run away. The Master demanded so much from them, so much more than seemed reasonable to ask of anyone. How could they measure up? When He told them that they were to be perfect as God is perfect (Matthew 5:48), they must have despaired. The demand is so large; the disciple is so small.

What magnetism Jesus must have had. In spite of His impossible demands, the disciples stayed with Him. They did more than that. When He gave them orders, they tried to obey Him, although their attempts at healing were often clumsy. Sometimes they failed, and their Master vented His exasperation. When they could not heal the epileptic boy (Matthew 17:14-20), His patience gave way: "O unbelieving and perverse generation, how long shall I stay with you? How long shall I put up with you?" When they asked Him why He succeeded in healing the boy after they had failed, He blamed their little faith. Then he brought up the mustard seed again: "I tell you the truth, if you have faith as small as a mustard seed, you can say to this mountain, 'Move from here to there' and it will move. Nothing will be impossible for you."

It seemed impossible, nevertheless.

"Because you have so little faith," Jesus chided them. Little faith in what? In this instance, too little faith in themselves as servants of the King of the kingdom. In both these little parables, Jesus chooses metaphors that suggest power in the objects themselves: the seed contains all that the mustard bush can become; the yeast contains power enough to transform the cells of the inert dough into which it is introduced. The seed and yeast do not have to do anything other than be what they were created to be.

Neither do we. Jesus does not demand superhuman feats of skill from us. He merely points that His kingdom is growing because it is its divine nature to grow. It is also the nature of the citizens of His kingdom to grow, enabled as they are by the Holy Spirit. Like the yeast, the citizens will transform their environments. All they need is the faith to be themselves in Christ and not give away to the fears that could stifle their growth.

"Faith," Charles Williams has written somewhere, "consists in the awareness that I am more than I know." You ought to memorize these words. I have. They remind me that I must not limit my possibilities to the confines of my past experiences or the norm of my friends and neighbors. When I gave myself to Christ and He gave himself to me, I became "more than I know." I can do more than I can do. "I can do everything through him who gives me strength" (Philippians 4:13). I may appear to you to be rather small and insignificant, and I may express myself rather immaturely upon occasion, but let me assure you, I am more than I seem.

Furthermore, the cause to which I have given my life, the kingdom of God on earth, may not yet rule the world, but don't discount it. It has lasted longer than any government on earth; it has become established on every continent; it has claimed every color of human skin; it has survived every attempt to annihilate it; and it is still growing. It is more than it seems to be.

Let me quote some encouraging words from George Mac-Donald:

"This is indeed a divine law! There shall be no success to the man who is not willing to begin small. Small is strong, for it only can grow strong. Big at the outset is bloated and weak.

There are thousands willing to do great things for one willing to do a small thing; but there never was any truly great thing that did not begin small.[4]

Jesus' contemporaries feared the Roman Empire. Never before had the world seen such majesty and might. How could they have guessed that in a few short centuries all that magnificence would be dust—and that the descendants of the tiny circle of Jesus' friends would be found all around the world?

Jesus entrusted His kingdom to this little band. He had faith in His disciples that they did not have in themselves. He knew what adversity lay ahead of them, but He also knew that strength grows in adversity. Like the old-timers in America today who boast of their exploits in the Great Depression while fearing that today's Americans have grown soft through prosperity, Jesus' disciples would never tire of telling of their sufferings for His sake, knowing that their suffering produced perseverance and their perseverance produced character (Romans 5:1-5). They chose not to surrender to their fears but to faith, faith in a growing kingdom and faith in their own growing. They did not remain immature indefinitely.

NOTES

[1]Copyright by United Feature Syndicate, Inc., 1981.

[2]Dag Hammorskjold, *Markings* (New York: Alfred A. Knopf, 1964), p. 93.

[3]Quoted by Robert E. Speer, *Five Minutes a Day* (Philadelphia: The Westminster Press, 1929), p. 35.

[4]*The World of George MacDonald,* Rolland Hein, ed. (Illinois: Harold Shaw, 1978), p. 150.

VIII. FORGIVE: YOUR LIFE DEPENDS ON IT

Matthew 18:21-35

A young lady went to see her doctor about her growing drinking problem. In the beginning, she drank only a little on the advice of another physician. Before long, she was drinking heavily and had discovered, to her horror, that she had become addicted.

Her doctor was not content to treat her symptoms. He sought the cause of her dependence. After two long talks, he still hadn't discovered it. Before they met for the third session, he spent an hour in prayer and meditation, seeking God's help. He still had no insight when they began their session. After a half hour, he suggested that they pray together silently before God. Then he mentioned a subject that had never come up: "Your mother."

She was surprised. Her mother was a saintly woman, against whom the daughter had no complaint at all.

Once again the doctor was disappointed. He hadn't helped, he thought. But that same evening, his patient telephoned him. "That's it," she told him. The more she thought about her mother, the more clearly she saw the problem. She admitted that she had always nursed a grudge against her mother *because* she was so saintly. She couldn't bear the burden of her mother's goodness. She had gone abroad as a governess in order to escape her mother; it hurt to be near her. She drank, the doctor had helped her to understand, as her way of subconsciously distancing herself even further from her mother's suffocating saintliness.

She then went to her mother to confess her hostility, threw her arms around her, and asked her forgiveness. When she forgave her mother, she gave herself new life. Her addiction was cured.[1]

New life depends on forgiving those who have done us wrong and, like this woman, those whose very virtue we resent because we feel we can't measure up to them.

More than once Peter had heard Jesus insist on forgiveness. "For if you forgive men when they sin against you, your heavenly Father will also forgive you. But if you do not forgive men their sins, your Father will not forgive your sins." Only as you forgive will you be forgiven (Matthew 6:14, 15).

It is a hard saying. Once again Jesus tangles our relationship with God up with our behavior toward other persons.

Not only must we forgive, but we must forgive and forgive and forgive. Up to seventy-seven times—or seventy times seven times, depending upon the manuscript you read. It doesn't matter which because both figures make the same point: just keep on forgiving—you'll never catch up with all that God has forgiven you.

THE SERVANT'S PLIGHT

As Jesus describes the servant's plight, it is a desperate one. The Lord exaggerates for emphasis, setting the servant's indebtedness at the equivalent of several million dollars, a staggering sum that the man could never repay in several lifetimes, in spite of his pitiful promise, "Be patient with me, and I will pay back everything." More than one sinner has prayed like this, unwittingly insulting God's intelligence by promising what could never be performed.

What no one can ever do is this: he can never repay God what he owes Him. You and I cannot "buy" forgiveness of sins. No plea bargaining will get us into Heaven; no matter how hard we work, we will never earn enough credits to buy our release as we stand before the Judge of the universe. We are lost without the Master's grace.

THE MASTER'S GRACE

The only escape for the servant is for the Master to cancel his debt and let him go. The Master takes the debt upon himself, assuming the servant's obligations and "taking a beating" in order that the servant might live. As the late Dag Hammarskjold has written, "Forgiveness breaks the chain of causality because he who forgives you out of love takes upon himself the consequences of what you have done. Forgiveness, therefore, always entails a sacrifice."[2]

That explains the cross of the Christian gospel, doesn't it? Sacrifice was needed for forgiveness to be possible. Only the cross can depict how Jesus could so freely forgive the most notorious of sinners—even His own executioners. Sin, the kind of sin Jesus is speaking of in this parable, always hurts the innocent. In this case, the servant's enormous debt burdens the innocent Master, who must suffer the staggering loss for him. Sin does that: it inflicts suffering on those least deserving of it. That is why it is up to the innocent to forgive. Only the injured one lifts the guilt of the injurer. Only God, therefore, can forgive man's sins against Him. That is the message of the cross: God is taking the beating on our behalf, grace replacing guilt, death exchanged for life. "This is love: not that we loved God, but that he loved us and sent his Son as an atoning sacrifice for our sins" (1 John 4:10). "Be kind and compassionate to one another, forgiving each other, just as in Christ God forgave you" (Ephesians 4:32).

THE SERVANT'S SEVERITY

The real contrast in Jesus' story is between the Master's grace and the servant's severity. If Jesus is telling the truth, then we actually have less to fear at the hands of God than of men. We frequently hear grumbling about the injustice of a God who could allow this or that to happen. Yet as I become more experienced in the ways of this world, my question has less to do with God than with men. God's ways seem merciful in the extreme when contrasted with the brutality of the human race.

Not long ago, I visited the horrible Nazi concentration camp at Auschwitz. Although I had read of it for years and had seen the horrors of the holocaust in films, I was still stunned as my companions and I trudged around the camp. Four million people had died there, victims of Nazi paranoia. I stared at the piles of hair clipped off victims herded into the gas chambers; I wondered at the huge piles of spectacles, shoes, suitcases, and other reminders that these were real people tortured here. We studied the crematorium, the gas chambers, the electric fences, the filthy sleeping mats, the ugly orderliness of this huge factory of death. With each new exhibit, my depression increased. Finally, when it seemed I could take in no more, I mumbled to my friends, "How long will God put up with us?" Why hasn't there been another flood to wipe us off the face of the earth, or a replay of the destruction of Sodom and Gomorrah, only this one final and universal? Don't speak to me of the severity of God after I have been to Auschwitz. That concentration camp is just one more proof of the depravity of godless humanity, like the Tower in London with its display of ingenious torture devices, like the multiplied slaughters in the Middle East, or even like the now tranquil battlefields in America where countrymen once butchered each other.

Why *does* God put up with us? What must He think when even His so-called representatives repudiate His grace and resort to bloodshed? Early in our civil war the session of the New York East Methodist Conference was opened with this prayer:

"Let the forces that have risen against our Government, and Thy law, be scattered to the winds. Grant, O God, that those who aimed at the very heart of the republic may be overthrown. We ask Thee to bring these men to destruction, and wipe them from the face of the country. . . ."[3]

He is the servant in Jesus' story all over again, forgetting what God's grace has done for him while demanding justice for others!

THE MASTER'S JUSTICE

The Lord, who is rich in mercy, can become the God of justice when justice is demanded of Him. But that is not His preference. He will be just only when He is forced to be. He prefers mercy.

When someone complains of God to me, grumbling of this or that supposed action of God, "It's not fair," I recall the words of a wise friend who warned me years ago that if I expected fairness in this world, I was doomed to disappointment. I also thank God that justice is not the standard He chooses to use in His relations with us. If He were to deal fairly with me, given my record, I would be undone!

The servant demands justice. He wants what is coming to him from his debtor. What he doesn't take into account is his master's sense of fair play. The master grants the servant's request: you want the standard to be justice, justice it will be. "In anger his master turned him over to the jailers until he should pay back all he owed." That's justice.

It is this demand for justice that fills our jails, clogs our court calendars, fills our war trenches, balloons our defense budgets—and kills our people. Demands for justice will never permit peace to reign in this tormented world. As I am writing these words, little wars (is there such a thing?) are in progress (strange, this coupling of the word *progress* with the word *war*) in South America, in Central America, in Europe, in the Middle East, in the Far East, and in many areas of Africa. The war cry is the same in each case: every nation claims to want nothing more than justice. At least, that is what their propaganda says. In the interests of justice, the inhabitants of planet earth are committing mass suicide. The whole human race is being "turned over to the jailers."

There is nothing impractical or dreamy-eyed about Jesus' demand for forgiveness. Only forgiveness, to quote Hammarskjold again, "breaks the chain of causality." Somebody must have the courageous grace to forgive somebody, or the Hatfields will go on feuding with the McCoys all over the world, until there is no world left to play host to the battles.

I met a radiant Christian woman in Poland a few years ago. What a brave soul. She had been a resistance fighter during Poland's German captivity during the Second World War. After the war, still wanting to fight for the best for her people, she joined the Communist Party. It seemed to offer the most hopeful solution to the nation's woes. Giving everything she could to the cause, she rose through the ranks of leadership to a position of prominence as a leader of Communism's youth in Warsaw. Even as she was gaining personal power, however, she was becoming disenchanted with the Party's broken promises and self-serving officers.

She sought a better solution. She found it in a little church of Christ in the city. She began attending services regularly, to the consternation of the Christians who did not know her motives. Like the Jerusalem Christians when the feared Saul of Tarsus showed up in their presence (Acts 9:26), these humble Polish Christians feared that they had a spy in their midst.

After attending and studying God's Word with these Christians, however, she became convinced that Christ was the solution she had been seeking. She presented herself to the elders for membership. The men delayed. They prayerfully consulted with one another, knowing the consequences to them and their church if she were there to destroy them. But they also knew the consequences to her—and to them—if they rejected an honest conversion. Finding courage in the Lord, they accepted her into membership. On the day of her baptism, several disbelieving Communists attended, their limousines lining the street outside the church building. They were incredulous that she should reject Marx for Christ. But she did. She has remained His faithful servant ever since. She had seen that Communism's promise of justice was leading to more bloodshed and more injustice. There was nothing in it to break the chain of causality. In Christ, she found something far better than justice; she found forgiveness and love.

When I saw this courageous woman, now in her last years, helping to feed her Communist-dominated country with food sent from Christians abroad, I thought of another remarkable woman of our century, Corrie ten Boom, whose *Hiding Place* in book and film has inspired millions. You know her story. The ten Booms lived quietly in Holland, repairing clocks, teaching children, and worshiping God. When the Nazis began their purge of the Jews, the ten Booms sheltered as many of the escaping Jews as they could. It was extremely dangerous. It was also fatal. The ten Booms were captured and sentenced to die in concentration camps. Corrie's father and sister never left the camps alive. She miraculously lived to tell her story.

After the war, this powerful Christian spoke in a Munich church concerning God's forgiveness. Following her message, she was startled to see one of her former guards approaching. He spoke to her, but she fumbled in her pocketbook, trying to avoid his eyes and his hand. She knew he wouldn't remember her among so many of his prisoners, but she certainly could never forget him. She could still see his leather crop swinging from his belt. What could she ever say to such a man?

He spoke first. He told her that he had been a guard at Ravensbruck, but then went on to say that since then he had become a Christian. He knew God had forgiven him for his former cruelty, but then he asked, with his hand outstretched, "Will *you* forgive me?"

Corrie knew she had no choice, in spite of her deepest feelings. She wanted to obey God in everything, and God demanded forgiveness. But Corrie had another reason. Since the war, she had run a home in Holland for victims of Nazi brutality. She had seen that the former prisoners who were able to forgive their enemies were able to rebuild their lives and return to the outside world. Those who held their bitterness in and refused forgiveness remained invalids. They did not heal. Corrie knew she had to forgive to live.

She also knew that forgiveness is not a feeling or emotion. It is a deliberate act of the will. Knowing that, she could pray, "Jesus help me," take the man's hand (woodenly at first, then with feeling), and say, "I forgive you, brother! With all my heart." They embraced, the former guard and his former prisoner. Something more wonderful than justice had been achieved.

God does not want to treat us with justice. He will, if we insist on it, but He prefers to forgive.

THE MEANING OF FORGIVENESS

Forgiveness is an act of will. It is a determination to forget. It remembers the sin no more.

The late great London preacher, W. W. Sangster, concluded a sermon on this theme with an illustration from his own home. A Christmas guest had arrived a couple of days early and saw the Christmas cards that Sangster was mailing. He was startled to see one name and address. "Surely, you are not sending a greeting to him," he said.

"Why not?" Sangster asked him.

"But you remember eighteen months ago. . . ." His guest began relating something the intended recipient had said about the preacher in public, something quite insulting. Then Sangster did remember the incident, but he also recalled resolving at the time that he would "remember to forget" the incident. God helped him, and he forgot.

He sent the card.

By the way, Sangster's sermon was on Genesis 41:51, "God . . . hath made me forget."

Forgetfulness is the essence of forgiving. Without it, no healing takes place—in the relationship or in the offended one.

When Andrew Jackson was President of the United States, he more than once promised his wife that when he had finished with politics, he would unite with a church. He admired the piety of his good wife. He even built a chapel for her on his Hermitage estate. He didn't get around to making his profession of Christian faith, however, until 1842, three years before his death. He explained the delay as a reluctance to give his political enemies a chance to say he had joined a church for political reasons.

As his minister examined him about his faith and experience, he asked, "General, there is one more question which it is my duty to ask you. Can you forgive all your enemies?" It was a fair question to ask a fighter whose career bristled with feuds, duels, battles, and personal animosities. He paused awhile, then said,

"My political enemies I can freely forgive; but as for those who abused me when I was serving my country, and those who slandered my wife . . . Doctor, that is a different case."

The minister wouldn't relent. He told him that a profession of faith meant little to one who harbored ill will against another. Another silence. Then at length, Jackson promised he would try to forgive all his enemies.

When he received communion, he touched the body and blood of Christ's forgiveness. Because of forgiveness, he could live.[4]

"While we were still sinners, Christ died for us" (Romans 5:8).

"Lord, how many times shall I forgive my brother when he sins against me? Up to seven times?" (Matthew 18:21).

NOTES

[1]Paul Tournier, *The Healing of Persons* (New York: Harper and Row, 1965), pp. 106, 107.

[2]Dag Hammarskjold, *Markings* (New York: Alfred Knopf, 1964), p. 197.

[3]Carl Sandburg, *Abraham Lincoln, the War Years,* Volume I (New York: Harcourt, Brace and Company, 1939), p. 220.

[4]Macartney, *Peter and His Lord* (Nashville: Abingdon-Cokesbury Press, 1937), pp. 60-62.

IX. GOD'S PERSONAL INVESTMENT PROGRAM

Matthew 25:14-30

I first met Tom Kirkpatrick in 1965. It was my first year on the job as Candidate Secretary for the Christian Missionary Fellowship. I had traveled to Brownsburg, Indiana, to interview Tom and Wanda, who had volunteered to become missionaries in Ethiopia.

I didn't know much about them. I knew that Tom was an elder in his church and that he was in a supervisory position with Allison Division of General Motors in Indianapolis. His wife was a leader in the missions department of the church. They were in their forties. That's all I knew.

Later I became acquainted with their two daughters, Susan and Sharon, as well as Sharon's husband Larry and their four children. On this visit, however, I concentrated on Tom and Wanda. Without theological education, with no overseas experience, with little practice in public speaking, with modest financial circumstances, this grandfather and his wife were offering themselves to serve the Lord in a land they had only heard of, on a mission that was not yet established.

What kind of people were they, anyway? Just ordinary folks, they insisted. Tom was a humble man, slow of speech, quietly doing his job, shying away from any attention to himself. For over twenty years, he punched his time-clock at Allison. At the same time, he was a faithful member of his church, taking care on this little task and doing that little assignment until his worth was acknowledged and he was elected to the church's eldership.

During those same years, Wanda distinguished herself as a mother and a leader among church women. She was largely responsible for the congregation's growing missions outreach program, praying about Christ's mission until He answered her prayers in the lives of the Kirkpatricks.

Tom and Wanda Kirkpatrick. Just ordinary Christian folks. One-talent people, they insisted. To me, however, they were a living dramatization of Jesus' parable, but with a difference. They took their one talent and made it pay for the Investor. God gave other people the ability to preach and sing and lead. God's gift to them was more limited, they thought. Their faith in Him was so strong, however, they trusted Him to make full use of what He had given them, wherever He chose to send them.

The result was that when Tom had died suddenly in 1982 of a rare disease, he was mourned on two continents by friends numbering in the thousands. After my visit with them in 1965, and we completed the necessary but frustrating preparations of missionary candidacy, Tom resigned his secure position in production control with G.M. and became a missionary in Addis Ababa. He saw himself not so much a missionary as a servant of missionaries. He was the liaison officer of the mission with the Ethiopian government. He ran the field missionaries' errands in the capital, banked their funds, kept their books, chauffered their children to boarding school, prepared their visas and other government papers, radioed them with information from the world outside their mission stations, dispatched Missionary Aviation Fellowship planes to rescue them in emergencies, and did a hundred other chores.

When the Communists ran Christian missionaries out of Ethiopia in 1977, instead of settling down in America for a much-deserved respite, Tom paced restlessly until he could return to his work, this time in Kenya. Time was short—and God needed whatever Tom could do for Him.

Then the illness struck. Tom quickly lost strength. He stayed at his desk until he could sit no longer. With quiet resignation, he returned to the States to die. Of him, it was also surely said, "Well done, good and faithful servant!" This man, his friends agreed, would surely hear the Lord say, "You have been faithful with a few things; I will put you in charge of many things."

I have told you about Tom because he is vivid proof of the timelessness of Jesus' parable. It is as modern as the ministry of Tom and Wanda Kirkpatrick.

Jesus was undoubtedly thinking immediately of His nation Israel, which had *not* exercised good stewardship of God's investment. The disciples of Jesus would have applied the parable to themselves, of course, for it, like so many of Jesus' other stories, reminded them of His high expectations of them. When we read the parable, however, we forget Israel or the disciples. The story is meant for us. Its moral is what God expects, what He gets, and what He does—about us.

WHAT GOD EXPECTS

It can be stated very briefly: God expects a good return on His investment. The principle that energizes Jesus' narrative is this: a servant belongs to his master; therefore all that he produces or earns also belong to his master. And the master expects to profit from his servant's labors.

No servant can say, "I am my own. What I do is my business. I am Number One in my life." He is not independent. He belongs to his master.

To compare God with a businessman may strike us as strange at first, but in this parable, Jesus doesn't hesitate to make such a comparison. He makes me think of a close business friend whose practices I have observed for more than twenty years now. Adhering to strict principles of integrity, he has managed to prove that honesty and success in today's business do not have to be mutually exclusive. On one principle of his operation, this honestly successful businessman never wavers: he expects a high return on any dollar he invests, or he can't be bothered with the proposal. He unsentimentally assesses any new venture for its potential return and sets a minimum percentage of return he feels he must have. In effect, he refuses to gamble. He is not afraid of calculated risks, but he calculates carefully.

God does the same, Jesus suggests. His parable's businessman gives three servants portions of his estate to manage. He apportions the responsibility according to his estimate of each servant's individual ability to manage. The reponsibilities are thus different, but the owner's expectation is the same. He wants each man to return the owner's investment plus profit.

The little story is encouraging, isn't it? Jesus implies that each of the servants, even the one-talent man, is worth something to the master. Each one is important, each one has a duty to perform, and each one will be morally responsible. Every servant is a worker, but more than a worker. He is also a contributor to the master's purposes. When he produces, he benefits his master, the business, and himself.

No worker can excuse himself because he feels inferior to another. Nothing more is expected of him than he can produce. Of course the five-talent man can produce five times as much; that is beside the point. What matters is whether the one-talent man is doing what he can. Strong or weak, he can produce. "For when I am weak, then I am strong," was the lesson the apostle

Paul learned the hard way (2 Corinthians 12:10). Even in sickness, his life could be used by God for His business.

In July, 1982, Don Bennett literally proved that weakness does not, should not, stop us from producing. Twelve years earlier, Bennett had climbed Mt. Rainier in Washington. It was a praiseworthy, but not terribly newsworthy, event. But when he returned in 1982, the press was watching, because this time the 52-year-old climber scaled the 14,408-foot mountain on one leg.

Two years earlier, Bennett had lost the other leg in a boating accident. He couldn't let his handicap keep him from reaching the top again. It was more important than ever that he succeed the second time. He had suddenly been reduced to a "one-talent" man, but through his weakness, he accomplished something he could never have achieved in his strength. Atop the mountain he planted some flags from contributors of the National Handicapped Sport and Recreation Association. For the sake of other handicapped persons, he reached the top.

I think Martha Berry's achievement no less astounding. This dynamic little lady asked Henry Ford for $1,000,000 for her rescue mission for boys and girls. He gave her a dime. Refusing to feel insulted, she put the dime to work. She had already given up her home in Georgia to take in every possible mountain boy and girl. She had no more room and not nearly enough equipment, but there was no shortage of needy children.

At least she had a dime. With it she bought a bag of peanuts and put her schoolboys to work planting them. The first crop was prolific, so she ordered that every nut be planted. The next crop was large enough to divide, half to replant, the other half to sell in bags at the nearby crossroads. Thus began her peanut business. Each year she made an accounting of all such sales until at last she could write Henry Ford in triumph: "Remember that dime you gave me? Well, Sir, I invested it in peanuts and now it has finally earned enough to buy a piano for our music students! How's that for dividends?"

Ford was impressed. He invited her to Detroit, treated her to dinner, and gave her the million dollars she had asked for years earlier. In the following years, he gave her further millions.[1]

Martha Berry had given Ford a huge return on his investment.

The discomforting question these examples and Jesus' parable force on us must now be asked, "What has God realized from his investment in us?"

WHAT GOD GETS

Sometimes He gets results; other times He gets excuses. The five-talent and two-talent men proudly presented the owner with the results of their stewardship. The timid one-talent man had nothing to give but alibis.

Results. There is no substitute.

From ancient Athens comes an oft-told tale of two men of that city who were being considered for some significant public work. In the tradition of Athenian democracy, each man had to speak before an assembly of citizens, presenting his qualifications for the assignment. The first speaker was a man of eloquence; with a flourish, he described the style in which the work should be done, his qualifications for doing it, and their pride in his achievement when the work was finished.

The next man was no speaker, but he got the job. "I cannot speak," he said, "but all that _____ has said, I will do." The citizens elected the do-er over the say-er. They wanted results.

When the late Senator Carl Hayden of Arizona was a freshman congressman, he was given this sage advice: "There are two kinds of Congressmen—show horses and work horses. If you want to get your name in the paper, be a show horse. If you want to gain the respect of your colleagues, keep quiet and be a work horse."[2] One kind gets the headlines, the other gets results.

Most work is routine, frequently dull, often politically and personally unrewarding. But without attention to the routine, without disciplined attention to details, lasting results can never be attained.

And God wants results.

What He more often gets are excuses. I am now middle-aged. There is no way around this incredible fact, even though my spirit accuses my calendar of lying. I've lived half my three-score and ten. I'm sliding down toward retirement years. Others are sliding with me. What I am noticing, to my chagrin, is that people my age develop an expertise that is not becoming to us. We are the master builders of excuses. Some of us are ingenious master craftsmen of deception. Most of us are dull imitators, offering nothing new. Just excuses and explanations and rationalizations—everything but results.

How God must tire of us. In Jesus' parable, the master asks the same of each worker. He provides the working capital. He has assessed each worker's potential. He does not ask more than what each is capable of, but he asks nothing less, either. Still, he gets excuses.

Abraham Lincoln had tried many good generals in his frustrating search for one who could win the Civil War for the North. Finally he called General Grant to Washington and gave him command. He had noticed that Grant had been winning victories on the western front. The general said little; he played no games with the journalists; he got a bad press—but he won. The secret of Grant's success could be explained, in part, by his response to someone who told him he should give the press the statement it requested about his objectives in his maneuvers around Vicksburg before the siege began. Grant characteristically grumbled, "This life is too brief to be frittered away with explanations."

He had no time to waste. He had a war to win.

God's faithful servants could offer as many excuses as the unfaithful steward. They, too, could have accused their master of being too demanding or even unfair. Nothing is easier than fabricating explanations for failure. But God wants results.

When a landslide in Darjeeling buried all six children of Mr. and Mrs. David Lee, they could have cried out against God's hardness. They could have yelled, "Foul," and refused to work any further for the Lord. But their lives were too short for explanations and recriminations. When their "little" family of six children was gone, they opened up a bigger home, with 300 children, and for sixty-five years cared for about that many. Mrs. Lee later said, "I've never had a sorrow in my life."[3] No explanations, no recriminations; just results.

WHAT GOD DOES

The parable is really about judgment. Our attention is drawn away from the servants to the master's judgment of his servants' management.

Two he approves. They have managed his property well. They will be rewarded with greater responsibility. They will share their master's happiness.

In Napoleon Hill's *How to Sell Your Way Through Life,* the famous salesman encourages his readers to play "a good joke" on their employers. He challenges them to get to work earlier and work later than required, to handle the boss's tools as if they were their own, to work at being kind to their fellow employees, to volunteer for the extra work that needs to be done. Then, he counsels, they should not show surprise when they are offered oversight of a department or partnership in the business. "This is the best part of the joke,"[4] he tells them.

Jesus would call that going the second mile on the job, wouldn't He? Paul would think of it as serving wholeheartedly, "as if you were serving the Lord, not men" (Ephesians 6:7).

I like William Ernest Hocking's advice: "In the course of a lifetime of imprudent undertakings, one maxim I have been led to adopt is that no task is to be evaded merely because it is impossible. The relevant questions are: whether it requires to be done, and whether the circumstances point a finger in one's direction."[5]

So take the job God offers and use the investment God has made in you to produce even more for the Boss. He will observe your management (stewardship). You'll enjoy your reward. He'll give you more to do.

Of one servant He disapproves. Offered excuses instead of results, the Lord has no choice but to strip the servant of any further responsibility. His fate is sealed. He will be deprived of his master's company. He had accused the master of harshness, but, in fact, it is he who had been unfair. He robbed the master of the interest he could have earned elsewhere.

No investor can afford a dishonest steward.

NOTES

[1]Margaret T. Applegarth, *Twelve Baskets Full* (New York: Harper and Bros., 1957), pp. 124, 125.

[2]Donald R. Matthews, "The Folkways of the U. S. Senate," *The Fiber of Democracy,* Wm. E. Brigman and John S. Vanderoef, ed. (San Francisco: Canfield Press [Harper & Row], 1970), p. 212.

[3]E. Stanley Jones, *A Song of Ascents* (Nashville: Abingdon Press, 1968), p. 182.

[4]Napoleon Hill, *How to Sell Your Way Through Life* (Cleveland: Ralston Publishing Co., 1958).

[5]LeRoy S. Rouner, *Within Human Experience: The Philosophy of William Ernest Hocking* (Cambridge: Harvard University Press, 1969), p. 67.

X. LIFE IS FULL OF SURPRISES—AND SO IS DEATH

Matthew 25:31-40; Luke 10:25-37

"Nothing is certain but death and taxes." This bit of conventional wisdom from Benjamin Franklin's Poor Richard seems wiser every generation, doesn't it? What is certain about taxes is that we shall pay them; what is certain about death is that we shall not escape it. Because of death's inevitability, we nurture an insatiable curiosity about it. What's to become of us? How long can we put it off? What's to become of our friends who are not of our religion? Is there really a Heaven or a Hell? Is there such a thing as "the Judgment"?

Jesus does not dodge the issue. Yes, death is certain. Yes, there will be a Judgment and God will be the Judge. His standard of judgment will differ from ours. Many people will be surprised.

SURPRISED AT THE JUDGMENT

When the Son of Man comes, He will divide the nations before Him—to the surprise of many persons in both groups. They will find their station in life to be no guarantee of their destination beyond. The cunning politician Machiavelli perceived at least that much about the Judgment. On his deathbed he remarked, "I desire to go to Hell, not to Heaven. In Hell I shall enjoy the company of popes, kings, and princes, but in Heaven are only beggars, monks, hermits, and apostles." A rather dull crowd for a career schemer.

Machiavelli had the same insight as Mark Twain's Huckleberry Finn. In this famous novel, Widow Douglas' sister, whose chief delight in life seemed to be to nag the hapless Huck into shape, told him all about the bad place. He said he wished he was there. Then she really got mad. "She said it was wicked to say what I said; said she wouldn't say it for the whole world; *she* was going to live so as to go to the good place." That didn't impress Huck a little bit. "Well, I couldn't see no advantage in going where she was going, so I made up my mind I wouldn't try for it."

Miss Watson just might be surprised at the Judgment.

Mark Twain mused often about death and its consequences, as in this widely circulated anecdote. He was attending a large dinner party once, and sat there in unaccustomed silence as the guests talked about eternal life and future punishment. Finally one of the guests asked Twain, "Why do you not say anything? I would like to hear your opinion."

Twain responded with solemnity, "Madam, you must excuse me. I am silent of necessity—I have friends in both places!"

I wonder how he knew who was where.

According to Jesus' parable of the sheep and the goats, there will be many surprises. The righteous, confident of their doctrinal purity, their punctuality in observance of the rituals, and perhaps their love of their own kind, will find that the Son of Man has something else in mind. God will separate on the basis of compassion. Kindness shown to the needy and helpless will be treated as offerings to Christ himself.

In Jesus' story, you can hear Old Testament prophets calling God's people back to His criterion of compassion. Deeds of justice and mercy must take priority over anything else. It does not impress God for us to observe days of fasting and sacrifices if we abuse our workers and neglect widows and orphans.

"Is not this the kind of fasting I have chosen:
to loose the chains of injustice,
    and untie the cords of the yoke,
to set the oppressed free,
    and break every yoke?
Is it not to share your food with the hungry,
    and to provide the poor wanderer with shelter—
when you see the naked, to clothe him,
    and to turn away from your own flesh and blood?
Then your light will break forth like the dawn,
    and your healing will quickly appear;
then your righteousness will go before you,
    and the glory of the Lord will be your rear guard.
Then you will call, and the Lord will answer;
    you will cry for help, and he will say: Here am I."
                                        Isaiah 58:6-9

When Jesus answers a clever lawyer's taunt, "And who is my neighbor?" with his immortal parable of the Good Samaritan, he closes the last loophole. The lawyer correctly summarizes the law: "Love the Lord your God with all your heart and with all your soul and with all your strength and with all your mind," and, "Love your neighbor as yourself" (Luke 10:25-37). The lawyer is conversant with loopholes, however, so he presses Jesus. Everything depends on the Lord's definition of *neighbor*. If He will agree that the word means one's family and the people who live nearby, or even that it means one's tribe or nation, then the lawyer can confidently face the Judge one day. But if neighbor means more—and Jesus makes it signify much more—then the lawyer has reason to fear.

Jesus forces the lawyer to admit that the merciful one demonstrates true neighborliness. The Samaritan's quickness to show mercy to someone he has never met before, perhaps of a different race, someone whose desperate plight would cost his benefactor time and money and would place him in acute danger of attack from the same robbers, is more than an impulsive act. It is the natural expression of the Samaritan's character.

Character is what another famous Biblical personality lacks (Mark 10:17-22). A rich young community leader, as concerned as the lawyer about his eternal salvation, leaves Jesus in dejection. Jesus has suggested that he give up his wealth for the sake of the poor. Never before has anyone challenged his religious sincerity by implying that he should trust the Lord instead of his wealth. Trapped by his possessions, he is not free to follow the Lord.

In both these passages, Jesus is consistent with his teaching in the parable of the sheep and goats. There will be a final judgment, and the Judge will separate mankind on the basis of faith expressed in compassionate deeds. If someone claims to believe in the Son of Man but does not love those whom the Son loves, his faith is fraudulent.

Faith in Jesus and love of others are inseparable. "Love one another as I have loved you," Jesus has taught us (John 15:12). The apostle John adds, "Whoever does not love does not know God, because God is love. This is how God showed his love among us: He sent his one and only Son into the world that we might live through him" (1 John 4:8, 9).

If we do not love, even the most pious among us will be surprised at the Judgment.

SURPRISED BY THE NATURE OF LOVE

Read 1 John 4:9 again. God sent His Son into the world as His act of love. But John 1:11 reports that He who came in love to His own people was rejected by them. Yet He refused to quit loving. Even as they were killing Him, He loved them enough to forgive them. Love does not have to be reciprocated. Love "always protects, always trusts, always hopes, always perseveres. Love never fails" (1 Corinthians 13:7, 8).

This is what so surprises both the "sheep" and the "goats." They would not have defined Jesus' list as acts of love. Charity (by our modern definition), perhaps, or mercy, or just doing what any decent person would do, but not love. The motive force of these acts, however, is the human equivalent of God's love in sending His Son. ("For God so *loved* the world that he gave . . ." John 3:16.)

Our contemporary confusion rests in what we have done to *love*. What can you expect from people who feed on huge doses of something called "love" in popular songs, television and radio soap operas, pulp magazines, romantic poems, and movies on this theme as different as G from X? How can we be expected to know that love can be an act of will that is not dependent on the object loved, that it can be expressed even when it is never returned, that it can be extended to strangers and prisoners and lepers?

Consider John Hinckley, Jr. He tried to kill President Reagan and managed to cripple permanently the President's press secretary because, said Hinckley, he *loved* actress Jodie Foster. Who taught him that homicidal behavior could even remotely be related to love? Everybody did! Everybody, that is, except Jesus. There is nothing sentimental, violent, or possessive in Jesus' love. If ever there was a clear-eyed view of this badly abused word, it was His. "Greater love has no one than this, that one lay down his life for his friends" (John 15:13). Not, as Hinckley would protest, that a man lay down someone else's life for his own.

I think Jesus would approve of George MacDonald's treatment of the subject: "To save man or woman, the next thing to love of God is the love of man or woman; only let no man or woman mistake the love of love for love!"[1]

When entertainer Sammy Davis, Jr., repudiated his Christian faith and became a Jew, a surprised nation asked him why. "As I see it," he announced, "the difference is that the Christian religion preaches love thy neighbor and the Jewish religion preaches justice, and I think justice is the big thing we need."[2] Had the disciples of Jesus done through the centuries what Jesus asked us to do, Davis would not have been driven from the Christian fold. The demand for human justice is as much at the heart of the Christian ethic as love is. Justice is love in action; it is love applied with impartiality. According to Jesus, you cannot separate love from justice without damaging both. But because justice keeps eluding us, love, which is more elastic and capable of greater mercy, must do more, not less, than justice. It wasn't justice that brought Jesus to us, but love. "But God demonstrates his own love for us in this: While we were still sinners, Christ died for us" (Romans 5:8). Only love could have so acted.

It is our response to the love of God, then, that compels us to love others. Such was the lesson a wise old rabbi was trying to teach his adoring but shallow disciple.

"My master, I love you!" the disciple blurted out one day.

"Do you know what hurts me, my son?" the venerable master asked him.

The young man was puzzled and offended. "I don't understand your questions, Rabbi. I am trying to tell you how much you mean to me, and you confuse me with irrelevant questions."

The rabbi assured him his question was neither confusing nor irrelevant. "For if you do not know what hurts me, how can you truly love me?"[3]

Jesus teaches something similar to His disciples. "Not everyone who says to me, 'Lord, Lord,' will enter the kingdom of heaven, but only he who does the will of my Father who is in heaven" (Matthew 7:21). What is His will? That we know what hurts Him and do something about it. Or, should we say, that we know whose hurting hurts Him and do something about them?

Love is active, not passive. It searches for the unloved and fills their longing. It sides with the outcast, the underdog, the confused who find this world too complicated for them. Love will be misunderstood, even hated ("If the world hates you, keep in mind that it hated me first," John 15:18), but it does not allow what others do to dictate its behavior. Love acts; it does not simply react.

When the famous preacher S. Parkes Cadman died, another famous preacher reminisced in his eulogy of the great man. Dr. Dan Poling recalled how, as a young minister, he had called on Dr. Cadman in his Brooklyn study and complained about the many hypocrites and spiritual loafers in his church. "I know, I know," the older man told him, "but if you want to help them and save yourself, you'll have to learn to love them, my boy."[4] That was all the advice he gave, Poling recalled, but that was enough. It taught him to *act* in love, not *react* to unloveliness in others.

This is the surprising toughness of love. It does not bend when abused, it does not depend on its goodness being returned. Love deliberately seeks out and assists those who cannot repay.

This tough love will be the basis of the examination on Judgment Day. The test results will be surprising.

SURPRISED BY THE KNOWLEDGE OF GOD

The examination will be very brief, because the Son of Man already knows the results. He has seen all along what we have done "to the least of these." God's eye is on the sparrow—and on our treatment of the sparrow. God takes even our little acts of kindness—or the absence of them—seriously, weighing them with eternal significance.

His watchfulness surpises even those who think they know Him best. I wonder what He thinks of their presumptuousness. The famous medieval mystic, St. John of the Cross, has written, "There is nothing in the world to be compared with God and he who loves any other thing together with Him wrongs Him." Where did he get that idea? He may be famous, but he is wrong. "If anyone has material possessions and sees his brother in need but has no pity on him, how can the love of God be in him?" (1 John 3:17). Doesn't this sound like loving God *and* another? What about this?

"No one has ever seen God; but if we love each other, God lives in us and his love is made complete in us. . . . For anyone who does not love his brother, whom he has seen, cannot love God, whom he has not seen. And he has given us this command: Whoever loves God must also love his brother" (1 John 4:12, 20, 21).

God's Word could not make it plainer. We can love God through loving others. There is real danger, in fact, in concentrating exclusively on Him, trying to fashion a "me and God and nobody else" religion. That is the root of hatred. It is the attitude that caused Jonathan Swift to write, "We have just enough religion to make us hate, but not enough to make us love one another."

When E. Stanley Jones, the missionary to India, was about to go to Manchuria, the Chinese pastors of Mukden wrote to him with his instructions: "Please do not preach to us to love our enemies, but preach to us spiritually."[5] An impossible assignment. In Scriptural terms, there is nothing more spiritual than the love of God expressed through His believers. His love is precisely the love of enemies.

The biggest surprise at the Judgment, perhaps, will be that God has kept no secrets from us. He will be exactly what His Word has revealed Him to be: He will be like Christ. His judgments will be according to Christ's Word (John 12:48), so it pays us to take Him seriously.

If we are surprised, it will not be His fault.

NOTES

[1]*The World of George MacDonald,* Rolland Hein, ed. (Illinois: Shaw Publishing, 1978), p. 82.

[2]Joseph Fletcher, *Situation Ethics* (Philadelphia: The Westminster Press, 1966), pp. 91, 92.

[3]Madeleine L'Engle, *Walking on Water* (Illinois: Shaw Publishing, 1980), pp. 70, 71.

[4]Dawson C. Bryan, *The Art of Illustrating Sermons* (Nashville: Abingdon Press, 1938), pp. 110, 111.

[5]*Christ's Alternative to Communism* (Nashville: Abingdon Press, 1935), pp. 48, 49.

XI. ALWAYS PREPARED

Matthew 25:1-13

I almost entitled this chapter, "Plan for Success." I like the sound of it better than the one I finally chose, but my conscience overruled. "Always Prepared" is much closer to the real intent of Jesus' parable, so it had to win, but "Plan for Success" points to the parable's extended application. Be prepared for the return of Christ. That is the moral of the story. But Jesus suggests far more, doesn't he? Preparation is not just for Christ's coming, but is an essential ingredient in anybody's recipe for success.

In the end, I decided I must talk about both. First, Christ's intent in telling the parable, and then its application to successful living.

BE PREPARED FOR THE LORD'S COMING

Once again Jesus draws on a wedding feast to describe something of the kingdom of Heaven. This was not a new idea to Jesus' audience. The Old Testament uses the same language for God's relationship with Israel: He's the bridegroom or husband, and Israel is His bride or wife (Hosea 2:16; Isaiah 54:6; Ezekiel 16:8f), although not always a faithful one.

The New Testament picks up the analogy and applies it to Christ and His church. He is the "husband" and the church is to be a "pure virgin" for Him (2 Corinthians 11:2). "Christ loved the church and gave himself up for her" so that she might be a perfect wife (Ephesians 5:25f). The church is a bride ready for her husband, the Lamb of God (Revelation 19:7).

In Jesus' parable, the bride awaits the groom, according to Jewish custom, at her home with her friends. These bridesmaids will join the friends of the groom in escorting the couple back to the groom's house, where the wedding feast will begin. Jesus doesn't mention the bride, by the way. Departing slightly from the usual Biblical language, in this case, He treats the bridesmaids as members of the church. In this respect, they resemble the wheat and tares, and the good and bad fish, in other parables. The bridesmaids are not necessarily good and bad, however, just prepared and unprepared.

All the maids sleep, although the moral of the story is watchfulness. "Preparedness" might be a preferred word, perhaps, since Jesus uses "keep watch" to mean " 'be prepared,' so when you see the groom and his party coming, everything will be ready."

Be prepared for another reason. The careless virgins do what all thoughtless people do in the moment of crisis: they try to force their friends to bail them out. "Give us some of *your* oil; our lamps are going out." *You* assume the responsibility for *us*. It's the cry of the weak and immature of every generation; smokers who expect insurance policies or government assistance to pay their self-incurred medical bills; chronic drinkers who expect family and employers and everyone else to take over their responsibilities; addicts who seek escape through drugged reveries, leaving the running of society to others; simple careless people who have learned that there is always someone else to pick up the ball when they drop it.

Jesus does not seem disposed to coddle the irresponsible. "No," the prepared maids seem to have answered. "You take care of yourself. Our provisions are not ample enough for us and for you as well."

For the unprepared, the wedding feast is not available.

For the prepared, the joy to be experienced is the stuff of which the angels sing:

"Then I heard what sounded like a great multitude, like the roar of rushing waters and like loud peals of thunder, shouting:

'Hallelujah!
    For our Lord God Almighty reigns.
Let us rejoice and be glad
    and give him glory!
For the wedding of the Lamb has come,
    and his bride has made herself ready.
Fine linen, bright and clean,
    was given her to wear.'

. . .Then the angel said to me, 'Write: "Blessed are those who are invited to the wedding supper of the Lamb!" ' " (Revelation 19:6-9).

The parable of the wedding feast is nestled in Matthew 25 between Jesus' discourse on the signs of the end of the age (chapter 24) and His parables of the talents and of the sheep and the goats. He has the future on His mind. One day, a day only God knows for certain, there will be an accounting of all people before the righteous Judge. The final separation will take place like the dividing of sheep from goats. In light of these future events, Christ's disciples must think of themselves as aliens living in occupied territory, awaiting their Liberator. They must be watchful, always alert to danger and to the joyful heralding of their Master's return.

Always practical, Jesus does not invite speculation on the day or hour of this day of liberation. In fact, He specifically forbids it (Matthew 24:36-44). He insists that His followers experience normal lives, living expectantly but without anxiety about tomorrow. Let the believer use his talents for God's glory, let him busy himself in feeding the hungry, clothing the naked, and doing other acts of mercy in Jesus' name, but let him never fall into idle speculation about times and seasons. It is sufficient to live so that whenever the Liberator comes, the believer is prepared.

In Poland, I met a charming old pastor who learned first hand what it means to be an alien in one's own country. During the Nazi occupation of Poland, Pastor Sascewiecz and his wife dwelt in a small apartment house. Above them, below them, and around them lived German soldiers with their families. Down the street in either direction were police stations. The Sascewieczes were surrounded.

The Nazis prohibited Polish people from worshiping in their own language. (Even the Nazis had to acknowledge the power of the gospel!) Nevertheless, Pastor Sascewiecz and his wife defied the ban. For several years, they conducted worship in their apartment for a couple dozen Polish Christians. During the week, the Sascewieczes sang hymns as loudly as they could—earning the nickname the "singing Sascewieczes" from the Germans— so that all the Christians could sing together softly on Sundays. It took the group about two hours to assemble as the Christians stealthily came, one by one, for the meeting. Then they took another two hours to leave, just as unobtrusively.

They were very watchful, these Christians. They prepared themselves for whatever would happen. They looked to the West for the day when their liberators would overthrow the Nazis and set them free. They looked beyond the West to the Highest, from whence one day the Lord himself would come. The liberation from the Nazis would be but a foretaste of the great release to come when the Lord would claim His own.

There has probably been no period of Christian history when the Lord's Second Coming has not been expected. But with the exception of the first century and the late tenth century, probably no other time has been as intensely interested as our own. Some Christians may claim indifference to the subject, but the statistics of book and magazine buyers prove them to be in the minority among conservative believers.

The Bible encourages us to anticipate the day when a new Heaven and a new earth will replace this battlefield of ours. Some of us seem more panic stricken than eager, however, preparing for self-preservation with an unbecoming heartlessness. The Philadelphia *Inquirer's* magazine *Today*[1] presents the shocking results of a survey of plans Christians are making for the end of the age. One man boasted that he had just purchased a .38-caliber snub-nosed pistol and is in target practice. He wants to be prepared to discourage people who will try to get his food. That's the way to take care of the unprepared! Other Christians are urged to retreat to mountain hideaways. They have stockpiled weapons, water, food, and quantities of gold and silver.

It is difficult to reason with panicky people. Jesus urged watchfulness, not cruel selfishness. Unfortunately, today's craving for more information about the end times (Hal Lindsey's *Late Great Planet Earth* has sold more than eighteen million copies—including thirty-one foreign editions.) has driven people to prepare for their physical survival, but it has had little effect on their spiritual readiness. That is the reason this parable must be read in the context of chapters 24 and 25. The parable of the sheep and goats is as critical to our understanding of the last days as is Jesus' warning in the parable of the ten virgins.

It is important to be prepared for Jesus' return. It is just as important to cultivate the habit of planning ahead.

BE PREPARED—PERIOD

During the agonizing days of Watergate, many brilliant men plotted their own political destruction. In the name of national security, they destroyed their personal security. Jeb Magruder was one of them. Like many of his cohorts, he later explained himself in a book. His was one of the better biographies to come out of Watergate. *An American Life: One Man's Road to Watergate* recounts the naivete of the bright young men in President Nixon's service.

"I think most of us who were involved in Watergate were unprepared for the pressures and temptations that await you at the highest levels of the political world. We had private morality but not a sense of public morality. Instead of applying our private morality to public affairs, we accepted the President's standards of political behavior, and the results were tragic for him and for us."[2]

Unprepared. Unprotected. Unqualified to stand against the fierce temptations of Washington. Magruder blames his fall on his generation's ambition to succeed personally and materialistically at any cost. Moral and ethical values did not receive the same priority. Men highly educated, personally attractive, showered with awards and accolades, had everything going for them but this: they lacked what a more old-fashioned age would call character. A little thing to this cynical age, perhaps, but essential nonetheless.

Old Benjamin Franklin was right after all: "For want of a nail the shoe was lost; for want of a shoe the horse was lost; and for want of a horse the rider was lost, being overtaken and slain by the enemy; and all for want of care about a horseshoe nail."

Attention to the little things can lead to incredible success. A junk dealer in the town of Mablethorpe, England, in eight years amassed enough savings to build homes for the aged. He was able to choose six old men and their families for his six bungalows and invite them to live in the houses without paying rent. "Twelve hours a day for eight years, pushing the cart around for junk—worth it, wasn't it?"[3]

He collected junk. From the little things other people had carelessly discarded, he could house six families. He worked hard, he saved diligently, he fulfilled his dream. He prepared for success by paying attention to little things.

Like Bjorn Borg, winner of five straight Wimbledon tennis championships. He had a dream, too: "I'd like to be remembered as one of the greatest players of all time."[4]

But dreaming didn't make it happen. Preparation did. As a ten-year-old kid, he'd hang around tennis courts, getting up at 6:30 and often being there until bedtime, waiting for his chance to get on the courts. Ten years old, and already preparing.

Of course, when you watched Borg play on television, you didn't see the preparation. He looked like a born champion, with his accurate lobs and incredible serves and famous two-handed strokes with a wrist action his coaches could never break him of. You never saw the long years of pure, hard, sweaty work that took him to Wimbledon. You didn't realize with what discipline he had mastered the little things that a less driven competitor would have overlooked. But when he retired in 1983, you knew he was, indeed, "one of the greatest players of all time."

There's something about the Christian faith in all this. Paul speaks of Christians as athletes (see Philippians 3:12-14) straining after a win. Preparation in Christian endeavors, no less than in athletics, means discipline, tedium, study, steadfastness, and scrimmages to get ready for the big contest. These are hard words for a success-oriented society like ours. We want instant accomplishment, immediate glory. We even blaspheme to the point of claiming that something that succeeds must be "of God." We don't discuss failure.

Jesus urges preparation. He does not promise everything will always go our way. Our business is to prepare, to do right, to love the Lord and our neighbors, to be diligent in fulfilling God's purposes for us. Our business is not to worry about the outcome. Even that master salesman of success in America, Zig Ziglar, recognizes this:

"Ability is important—dependability is critical. . . . The real opportunity for success lies within the person and not in the job; that you can best get to the top by getting to the bottom of things—and then climbing those stairs—one at a time."[5]

I may be dwelling too long on this application of Jesus' parable. I confess I am doing so because of some recent counseling sessions. They in turn have caused me to reflect on my years of trying to help people succeed. These sessions have driven me to an inescapable conclusion: most people in trouble are there because they have not prepared to get out of it. They never bothered to get a supply of oil for their lamps. They have not thought further than the impulse of the moment. They have not budgeted their money, planned their time, thought through their career choices, foreseen the long-term results of their child-rearing practices, prayed for wisdom, sought the counsel of sager heads before it was too late, or in any other way given thought to the crises that come like a thief in the night. "You do not know the day or the hour" when the Lord may come. You do not know the day or hour when just about anything may come!

On such an hour recently my telephone rang. John Hobbs,

sixteen-year-old member of our church youth group and my son's best friend, was dead. The gyro-copter he was flying lost power and plummeted to John's instant death. Sixteen years old and dead. What can you say to grieving parents, to your stunned son, to anyone?

This death was not as hard for us as some, because John, though only a teenager, had already given himself to the Lord. It showed in his life, too. Although not immune from a normal boy's daring curiosity, he was really growing in his faith and conduct. When he died, we all cried, but we could comfort ourselves with the knowledge that John was prepared.

The words of Jesus to the church at Sardis came to haunt me during the days following John's accident:

"Remember, therefore, what you have received and heard; obey it, and repent. But if you do not wake up, I will come like a thief, and you will not know at what time I will come to you" (Revelation 3:3).

The Apostle Paul uses similar language in his discussion of Jesus' second coming with the Thessalonians:

"Now, brothers, about times and dates we do not need to write to you, for you know very well that the day of the Lord will come like a thief in the night. While people are saying, 'Peace and safety,' destruction will come on them suddenly, as labor pains on a pregnant woman, and they will not escape.

"But you, brothers are not in darkness so that this day should surprise you like a thief. You are all sons of the light and sons of the day. We do not belong to the night or to the darkness. So then, let us not be like others, who are asleep, but let us be alert and self-controlled . . ." (1 Thessalonians 5:1-6).

Isn't this just another way of saying, "Be prepared"? Let me add one more, this time from Peter:

"Since everything will be destroyed in this way, what kind of people ought you to be? You ought to live holy and godly lives as you look forward to the day of God and speed its coming" (2 Peter 3:11).

Taken together, these Scriptures describe the suddenness of the Lord's coming, like the suddenness of death, by such terms as a "thief in the night," a "lightning flash," "the sound of the last trumpet." Something sudden, even catastrophic, and certainly decisive, is going to happen.

So be prepared.

NOTES

[1] April 12, 1981. Quoted in *Evangelical Newsletter,* May 1, 1981.

[2] Jeb Magruder, *An American Life: One Man's Road to Watergate* (New York: Atheneum, 1974), p. 349.

[3] From *The Saturday Review.* Quoted in Gerald Kennedy, *A Reader's Notebook* (New York: Harper and Brothers, 1953), p. 275.

[4] *Time* (June 30, 1980).

[5] Zig Ziglar, *See You at the Top* (Gretna, Louisiana: Pelican Publishing Company, 1975), p. 24.

XII. WHEN GOD DOESN'T GET HIS WAY

Matthew 21:33-46

Not everything that happens is God's will. As Jesus' Parable of the Tenants points out, even God's own people don't always do what He wants.

Yet Jesus is only one of many Biblical teachers who lament Israel's resistance to God's purposes. Listen to the discouraged conclusion of the chronicler:

"The Lord, the God of their fathers [Judah's], sent word to them through his messengers again and again, because he had pity on his people and on his dwelling place. But they mocked God's messengers, despised his words and scoffed at his prophets until the wrath of the Lord was aroused against his people and there was no remedy" (2 Chronicles 36:15, 16).

Nehemiah voiced the same complaint:

"But they [the Israelites] were disobedient and rebelled against you; they put your law behind their backs. They killed your prophets, who had admonished them in order to turn them back to you; they committed awful blasphemies. So you handed them over to their enemies, who oppressed them. But when they were oppressed they cried out to you. From heaven you heard them, and in your great compassion you gave them deliverers, who rescued them from the hand of their enemies.

"But as soon as they were at rest, they again did what was evil in your sight" (Nehemiah 9:26-28)

The writer of Hebrews eulogizes the great leaders of Israel, such men as:

"Gideon, Barak, Samson, Jephthah, David, Samuel and the prophets, who through faith conquered kingdoms, administered justice, and gained what was promised; who shut the mouths of lions, quenched the fury of the flames, and escaped the edge of the sword; whose weakness was turned to strength; and who became powerful in battle and routed foreign armies. Women received back their dead, raised to life again. Others were tortured and refused to be released, so that they might gain a better resurrection" (Hebrews 11:32-35).

And how did God's people treat these His servants?

"Some faced jeers and flogging, while still others were chained and put in prison. They were stoned; they were sawed in two; they were put to death by the sword. They went about in sheepskins and goatskins, destitute, persecuted and mistreated—the world was not worthy of them. They wandered in deserts and mountains, and in caves and holes in the ground" (Hebrews 11:36-38).

So God tried once more. Seeing his servants the prophets rebuffed so humilatingly, He sent His own Son. But even though "He came to that which was his own . . . his own did not receive him (John 1:11).

Obviously, God's will is not always done.

ISRAEL'S BETRAYAL

Jesus' Parable of the Tenants was not misunderstood by His critics. "When the chief priests and the Pharisees heard Jesus' parables, they knew he was talking about them" (Matthew 21:45). They looked for a way to kill him, as Jesus had just told them they would. Even the Son was not safe from the murderous hands of the tenants.

Matthew places this story just after Jesus' triumphant entry into Jerusalem. He comes with authority. Exercising the power of God's own Son, He drives hucksters and money changers from the temple area and heals the blind and lame. In order to dramatize God's impatience with His non-productive nation, Jesus curses a fig tree, which immediately withers from His scornful blast. When the temple leaders challenge His authority, He disdains to defend himself. The Son has no need to explain himself to lesser men. Instead, He tells a couple of stories, the first about obedient and disobedient sons, and this second one about a disobedient nation. He makes certain that His challengers understand that what Israel has done to the prophets and is about to do to Jesus is not God's will. They are not simply quieting a disturber of the temple peace; they are defying the Lord God himself.

When Jesus speaks allegorically of a landowner who planted a vineyard and turned it over to some tenant farmers, all the good Jews within hearing distance knew He was talking about their nation. He was borrowing heavily from the words of the prophet Isaiah (Isaiah 5:1-7):

"I will sing for the one I love
 a song about his vineyard:
My loved one had a vineyard
 on a fertile hillside.
He dug it up and cleared it of stones
 and planted it with the choicest vines.
He built a watchtower in it
 and cut out a winepress as well.
Then he looked for a crop of good grapes,
 but it yielded only bad fruit."

Isaiah leaves no doubt that he is speaking on behalf of God to His nation:

"Now you dwellers in Jerusalem and men of Judah,
 judge between me and my vineyard.
What more could have been done for my vineyard
 than I have done for it?
When I looked for the good grapes,
 why did it yield only bad?"

What should He do with a vineyard over which He has labored so diligently and profitlessly?

"Now I will tell you
 what I am going to do to my vineyard:
I will take away its hedge,
 and it will be destroyed;
I will break down its wall,
 and it will be trampled.
I will make it a wasteland,
 neither pruned nor cultivated,
 and briers and thorns will grow there.
I will command the clouds
 not to rain on it."

Then, to make doubly certain no one can miss his point, Isaiah adds,

"The vineyard of the Lord Almighty
 is the house of Israel,
and the men of Judah
 are the garden of his delight."

To Jews steeped in the traditions of the prophets, Jesus' simple allegory of the tenants in the vineyard can have just one interpretation: He's talking about us! And He's talking about himself. He says *He* is the stone we are tripping over. Worst of all, He's bullying us with threats that God will find another people to be the laborers of His vineyard.

So they plot his destruction—just as Jesus said they would.

Ever since the days of Moses, Israel prided itself in the special covenant God had made with His people. What Israel did not fully comprehend, however, was the distinctive quality of the relationship God wanted. Unlike the false gods of the nations, Israel's God was never to be regarded as the exclusive property of any one nation. That their God loved and cared for His vineyard the Israelites knew full well. But that He also loved all the nations of the earth and wished Israel to be His means of blessing them was a fact they but dimly recognized.

When He tried to return them to His purposes through His spokesmen, the prophets, they stoned and killed them. Consequently, Jesus forces the Pharisees to admit, "He will bring those wretches to a wretched end, . . . and he will rent the vineyard to other tenants."

Jesus doesn't add, but He could, that the wretches will then inevitably cry out against God for rejecting them.

What else can the God of blessings do when His agents for delivering the blessings won't work? Must He not turn to someone else?

In Victor Hugo's *Les Miserables,* the famous author explains Napoleon's incredible defeat at Waterloo in similar fashion. The whole European system Napoleon had forged crumbled away, not because of Wellington or Blucher, but because of God, who decreed that the French dictator should fall because "he embarrassed God." So had the tenants of the vineyard. They did more than that. They foiled His plans, ruined His harvest, impugned His character, killed His servants, and murdered His Son.

God doesn't always get His way. He has often suffered embarrassment. Even His own people betrayed Him.

MAN'S CRUELTY

Jesus' story must not be applied only to Israel, however. That's too easy, too tempting. Generations have done just that, of course, using the Jews as a covenient scapegoat for the ills of human society. But this is a cop-out. We can't blame the Jews alone. Not any more. Not after the Holocaust of World War II. Not after Vietnam. Not after Lebanon or El Salvador or Afghanistan or just about any nation's war you want to mention.

Anti-Semitism ignores one awful fact: we are as ready to kill the prophets and murder the Son as any Jews ever were. Why shouldn't we, after all, since we have been so willing to kill everyone else?

We are not dealing here with the specific crime of a specific nation, but with cruelty rooted in the very nature of humanity. What do we mean when we say, "I'm only human," if not that consistent ethical behavior is too high, too super-human for us? "Fighters against the will of God"—this could almost serve as a definition of humanity.

At least that's the way Mark Twain characterized us. "Adam was but human—this explains it all," he wrote somewhere. "He did not want the apple for the apple's sake; he wanted it only because it was forbidden. The mistake was in not forbidding the serpent; then he would have eaten the serpent."

We tenants in God's vineyard resent His authority. We will not do what we are told, we will not give Him His share of the harvest, we *will* kill rather than be dictated to.

We must take care not to speak too blithely of the sovereignty of God who rules in all things. He doesn't. He frequently doesn't even rule in my life, let alone in human affairs generally. I am like Elton Trueblood in having no doubt that God has a will for my life, but I am also like him in my certainty that I frustrate that will time and again. God made us free; unfortunately, "not only are we free to initiate action; we are also free to resist."[1]

We resist admittedly. Worse, we openly rebel against God and go to war against one another, especially against the representatives of God. "What ails us," P. T. Forsythe has written,

"is not limitation but transgression, not poverty but alienation. It is the breach of communion that is the trouble—the separation, the hostility. We are not His counterparts but His antagonists. . . . As a race we are not even stray sheep, or wandering prodigals merely; we are rebels taken with weapons in our hands."[2]

Left on our own, we chase one another around our circles with vicious intent. We demand the right to govern ourselves so that we can repress others. We fight for the right to enrich ourselves even when it means impoverishing others. We *will* have our comforts no matter how many we make uncomfortable in the process. We will protect our seats in the lifeboat while shoving the drowning away to their deaths.

It doesn't matter much which "-ism" we adopt, either. Communism may preach the equality of the masses, but the masses share none of the perquisites of the high officials. Capitalism can talk of equality of opportunity, but where is it really found? Militarism promises to solve all problems with guns, and academism with books, but the problems persist. Whether the cause is feminism or agism or hedonism, every "-ism" is structured to guarantee the welfare of the elite within and discrimination against the aliens without.

What will God do with such rebellious tenants?

GOD'S DETERMINATION

One thing is certain: He won't give up or give in to the rebels. From beginning to end, the Biblical message is sure: God is going to win. All your rebellions, your stonings, your murders, and your threats will come to nothing. When you fall on the stone (the Son, Jesus), you, not the stone, will be crushed. Trace the history of Israel. In the creation of Adam, in the rescue of Noah from the flood, in the call of Abraham from Ur, in rescuing captive Israel from Egypt, in the elevation of David to the throne, in the exhortations of the prophets, in the cross of Jesus, God's purpose remains the same: He *will* bless His creation. One way or another, He will bless. He will not wait for us to reform; He will bless so that we can reform.

"You see, at just the right time, when we were still powerless, Christ died for the ungodly. Very rarely will anyone die for a righteous man, though for a good man someone might possibly dare to die. But God demonstrates his own love for us in this: While we were still sinners, Christ died for us" (Romans 5:6-8).

He didn't wait. In spite of everything, He didn't wait. "This is love: not that we loved God, but that he loved us and sent His Son as an atoning sacrifice for our sins" (1 John 4:10).

It was His way of starting another vineyard, a new Israel, tended by servants who know themselves loved by the Owner and who want to return His love. These new servants are aware they have no inherited right to their jobs in the vineyard. They haven't earned their position through special connections or sterling personal qualities, either. They are there because God has loved them and they have accepted.

Let me change the picture a bit to say the same thing. In

Rome's catacombs, you can still see some ancient Christian drawings on the walls. One of the most frequent ones is of an ark floating upon the waters. The huddled Christians meeting in these dark tunnels thought of the church as a boat like Noah's; their evangelistic invitation was to drowning men and women to "come into the ark." They believed that godless humanity was being inundated in a flood of its own making; what the world needed most was the ark/church, which God designed for rescuing the lost.

The church's presence in the world today is constant proof of God's determination. He may be rebuffed and rejected, but He will keep on trying. So far, He has been patient with the none-too-faithful workers in this new vineyard. Let's hope He will hold on a little longer.

Robert Schuller succinctly defines the church in terms of its ministry: "The church is a group of happy, Holy Spirit inspired Christians—the body of Christ helping hurting people in the community."[3] There is more to be said, but Schuller is right in zeroing in on the church's ministry. It is to produce! It produces happy, Holy Spirit inspired Christians out of hurting people. It honors the Son by loving those He loves, saving those He wants saved, healing and giving hope and sacrificing itself in His name. It will remain God's church so long as it does God's will in blessing whom He would bless. He has often been disappointed—but He is still determined.

NOTES

[1]Elton Trueblood, *A Place to Stand* (New York: Harper and Row, 1969), pp. 88, 89.

[2]P. T. Forsythe, *Positive Preaching and the Modern Mind* (A. C. Armstrong and Son, 1907; Grand Rapids: Baker Book House, 1980), p. 56.

[3]Quoted by Marshall Leggett, "Reflections," *Christian Standard* (August 23, 1981), p. 4.

XIII. AT LAST, JUSTICE!

Luke 16:19-31

Of Jesus' many parables concerning the last Judgment, none is more famous than the tale of Lazarus and the rich man.

I have read it many times through the years, but never before this year has it made such an impact on me. I read it while on my visit to Poland that I have already mentioned. The contrast between this wealthy American and my impoverished Polish friends was almost more than I could bear. I am accustomed to shopping in supermarkets gorged with spectacular displays of food; my friends were making do with next to nothing. When they entertained my traveling companion Bob Walther and me in their homes, and we thanked them for the fine meal, they invariably replied, "But you must remember, it is your food."

That was true. Bob and I were in the country representing Christians of Encouragement, a spontaneous movement among some American Christians to raise money and food to ship to hard-pressed Poland. Without our aid and the aid of millions of other Westerners, the situation there would have been even more desperate than it was. We observed the long lines of people waiting in the hope—which more often than not proved to be a vain hope—that today they could purchase shoes for their children, or a piece of fabric, or an essential bit of food.

This was not the first time I had been in a financially depressed country. It was the first time, however, that I studied this parable surrounded by reminders of the contrast between others' poverty and my relative wealth. I knew—and I know—that the inequity between my much and their little cannot be right.

When Bob tried to give Pastor Sascewiecz, whom I mentioned in the last chapter, a pen as his gift from America, the kindly old saint protested, "Oh, I have." Since he already had one ball point pen, he could not in good conscience accept another. Too many of his countrymen had no pen. He should not collect what they could not have. I did not confess how many I had in my desk drawer at home.

The problem with being wealthy is ignorance, an ignorance that is often willful. The wealthy don't know and don't want to know how the poor exist. They are often like the matron who would put down her limousine's window shades when her chauffeur drove her through part of her city's slum district. She refused to allow her tranquility to be disturbed by sights that offended her sensibilities. No one who is given to dressing "in purple and fine linen" and living "in luxury every day" wants to know about beggars "covered with sores" pleading for scraps "from the rich man's table." His concern is with the care and feeding of the rich.

But Jesus' compassion is with the Lazaruses of this world. He does not give the rich man a name, but Lazarus is the only character in any of Jesus' parables to be given one. His name means "God helps." He alone cares that Lazarus is pitiful, that he ekes out an existence on the table droppings of the wealthy, too weak to shoo the dogs away from his ulcerated body.

It's unjust that two men, living side by side, should be so far apart. Jesus doesn't promise here—or anywhere else—that their disparate conditions will be equalized on earth. But there will be a turn-about eventually, when the men are weighed on the scales of eternal justice. God does not suffer such inequities forever.

To see the wrongs righted, however, we have to look beyond the confines of this earth.

THERE IS LIFE AFTER DEATH

If existence this side of the grave were all we had, we should despair indeed. The Saducees of Jesus' day were convinced that there is no afterlife. It was a comfortable doctrine for them, since for the most part they were the wealthy and prestigious class of Israel. Jesus may have had them in mind when He told this parable, a warning that their self-indulgence now would be evidence against them later. Their books would not be closed when they died; the final accounting would come in the afterlife.

Jesus never wavered in His teaching regarding life after death. "I am the resurrection and the life," he promised His disciples. "He who believes in me will live, even though he dies; and whoever lives and believes in me will never die" (John 11:25, 26). The God who was and is and will be may permit temporary inequities on this earth, but He will not allow them forever. Many who now are first will be last, and the last first (Matthew 19:30).

Have no fear, there is life after death! This promise is inherent in the gospel (1 Corinthians 15:1-8). Jesus lived, died, and rose from the dead. Those who are in Him will do the same (Romans 6:1-10). Then God's justice will replace man's injustice; then God's mercy will heal those maimed by human mercilessness.

I can't talk about this sublime subject without thinking of the rather irreverent story Jess Moody tells. He reports that when Stalin's body was removed from Red Square in Moscow, the Kremlin searched for a place to redeposit him in some more or less remote country outside the Soviet Union. They finally agreed that Israel would be the best place. They changed their minds, however, when an official in Jerusalem told them, "You are perfectly welcome to do this but we feel that we should tell you that here we have the highest resurrection rate in the world."[1]

That official had read the Gospels.

The parable does not argue for the resurrection of the dead, of course. Jesus just assumes it. He pictures the rich man and Lazarus resting in Hades, the abode of the dead, very much alive. But their former state has been reversed.

THERE IS JUSTICE AFTER DEATH

At last someone has taken pity on Lazarus. Justice has come. On earth, the poor yearn for justice, prophets preach about justice, courts struggle to arrive at justice, but what is accomplished is almost never justice. Our knowledge is too limited. But God's is not. He can and He will settle all accounts fairly.

At least some of Jesus' audience must have been surprised at the unique twist in His story. The dominant outlook in first century Judaism would have concluded that Lazarus was a miserable sinner who deserved to the punished by God. Like many a latter-day Christian, Jesus' contemporaries equated material success with God's favor and sickness and poverty as proof of sin in one's life. When Jesus sided with the beggar, He goaded them into looking again at their shallow doctrine of divine providence.

We must not read the parable, however, as a pitting of the rich against the poor. Jesus did not disparage wealth *per se*. What He criticizes is the failure of the rich to seize their opportunities to help the poor. It is the calloused selfishness of the purpled aristocrat that summons the Teacher's censure. The rich man couldn't leave his home without almost stumbling over the pitiful creature at his gate. Yet he did nothing.

So God must do something.

Too late the man faced up to the truth about himself. This is not a bad definition of hell, by the way. Thomas Hobbes said it in almost exactly these words: "Hell is truth seen too late." Cyril Connolly, a prolific writer and talker, offers a variation on the same theme: "My idea of Hell is a place where one is made to listen to everything one has ever said."[2] Hell is where I am forced to look at, to really see, and to listen and really hear, myself.

Sometimes we are vouchsafed a glimpse of such a review of our behavior. There's a well-known story of an alcoholic who brutally beat his son in his drunken passions. One day, when for a change the man was sober, the little boy was lying ill of such a high fever he became delirious. As his father leaned over his cot to comfort him, the little boy put his hands up in front of his face and screamed, "Don't let him hit me, Mommy." Only then did the father realize what he had been doing while he was drunk.

Only "in hell" was the rich man forced to see what he had been doing against Lazarus. And not only against Lazarus. Jesus is here dramatizing his consistent theme that love of God and love of man cannot be separated, for showing kindness to "One of the least of these brothers of mine" is showing kindness to Christ himself (Matthew 25:40). Stepping over Lazarus on the way to purchase more fine linens is like tromping on the will of God. To indulge oneself on exotic foods and drinks while someone else starves is as abusive as the drunken father beating his little boy. Self-worship is the crassest form of idolatry; it drives a wedge between the self and God. As the rich man had closed the gate between himself and Lazarus, now another barrier, "a great chasm," has been fixed between the tormented plutocrat and the comfortable Lazarus.

There is justice after death.

THERE IS NO HOPE FOR THOSE WHO CHOOSE TO DISBELIEVE

At last Dives (the rich man) thinks of someone else. He has five brothers. If only he can warn them. "I beg you, father, send Lazarus to my father's house." It was apparent that he couldn't go. He was surrounded by the chasm, denied the comfort of Abraham, cut off from the living. Perhaps the newly privileged Lazarus could go instead.

"No need to," Abraham tells him. "They haven't listened to Moses and the Prophets. They have ignored the voice of God through His representatives. They'll only ignore Lazarus as well."

We choose to believe; we choose to disbelieve. Ample evidence had been supplied; it had been ignored by the rich man, and it would be ignored by his brothers. Even a resurrection from the dead is not sufficient news to force them to listen. Their condition is hopeless, then, not because God wants to condemn—what an outrageous suggestion!—but because they have chosen to live without regard to the future or to God. A. J. Cronin has described Hell as "the place where one has ceased to hope." If that be true, then Hell does not start with death. Hopelessness sets in much earlier. To believe in no life after death, to live for pleasures of the moment because there is no tomorrow, to reject any notion of a God who rules life and afterlife, is to have no hope in a better tomorrow.

Dante, in *The Inferno*, placed over the gates of Hell the words, "Abandon hope, all ye who enter in." In fact, hope has long before been abandoned. That explains their entering in. The rich man had no hope in any future existence. Disbelieving in promises of a future more glorious than what his wealth could presently afford him, he isolated himself from God's other children. He dug the chasm between Abraham and himself. It was he, not God, who chose hopelessness. Death just granted the man the consequences of his choice.

FOR BELIEVERS, THERE IS EVERYTHING TO HOPE FOR

The meaning of Lazarus' name, you will recall, is "God helps." Lazarus could find no help on earth. He could only trust himself to God. God does not disappoint him. In the abode of the dead, he enjoys his position at the table, beside Abraham, in the honored place. He is there because, like the Father of the faithful, he placed his trust in the goodness of God, who would one day rescue him from the abuse of men.

Death offers Lazarus not only an alternative to his poverty and abuse, but also the healing of the terrible sores on his wretched body. He has gone to the abode where "there will be no more death or mourning or crying or pain" (Revelation 21:4), and the perishable body "is raised imperishable" (1 Corinthians 15:42). In hope, believers endure physical ailments in this life, anticipating wholeness in the life to come.

Robert Berry wrote a moving testimony to his father's faith. The elder man's chemotherapist asked him what he planned to do about chemotherapy, without which "you've sealed your fate."

Doctor, I believe in God and I read His word. The Bible says, "The days of our years are three-score and ten." I've lived sixty-six wonderful years. If I die now, I've only missed that mark by four years. Sure it will be hard on my wife and family, but God put me on this earth for a purpose. My wife and I raised three boys. We brought them all up to believe in Christ and they all have college educations and have good Christian families of their own. Now God's purpose for my life on this earth is coming to a close.

I believe in life after death. I believe that when this earthly body is worn out, it is cast aside and God gives us a heavenly body. I would like to live my last days on this earth as comfortably as I can. I don't want to run the risk of being so sick for whatever time I have left that I couldn't enjoy the company of my wife, children, and grandchildren. I appreciate what you have to offer, but I just feel that what God has to offer is a lot more certain.[3]

So he refused chemotherapy, anticipating a far better healing later on.

In this respect, he shared the faith of Elizabeth Barrett Browning. As her son Pen's playmate lay dying, she sat beside the boy's grieving mother and wrote her, "I can't look on the earthward side of death. I flinch from corpses and graves. When I look deathwards, I look over death upwards."[4]

So do all who hope in God. This is the upward look of the apostle Paul, who described his life on earth as a battle or strenuous contest. He had no doubt about his reward, however.

"Now there is in store for me the crown of righteousness, which the Lord, the righteous Judge, will award to me on that day—and not only to me, but also to all who have longed for his appearing" (2 Timothy 4:8).

He who had been sickly, beaten, persecuted, worried, tormented, and jailed in his service for Christ had no fears about his future.

"Now we know that if the earthly tent we live in is destroyed, we have a building from God, an eternal house in heaven, not built by human hands. Meanwhile we groan, longing to be clothed, with our heavenly dwelling, because when we are clothed, we will not be found naked" (2 Corinthians 5:1-3).

Although we suffer, we do not despair. To the contrary, we are confident. One day, everything will finally be put in order.

Wrongs will be righted, good will be vindicated. "For we must all appear before the judgment seat of Christ, that each one may receive what is due him for the things done while in the body, whether good or bad" (2 Corinthians 5:10).

At last, justice.

NOTES

[1]*Don't Miss It If You Can* (Waco: Word Books, 1965), pp. 124, 125.

[2]Quoted in "New Books," *Saturday Review* (January 25, 1975), p. 41.

[3]Robert W. Berry, "My Most Memorable Sermon," *Christian Standard* (June 15, 1980), p. 8.

[4]*Halford Luccock Treasury*, Robert Luccock, ed. (Nashville: Abingdon Press, 1963), p. 309.

LEROY LAWSON
SHARES THE SECRET

The secret of living an extraordinary life. In *The Lord of Promises,* you will learn how to claim thirteen of Jesus' most powerful promises as your own! Order #39989 (Instructor, #39988).

———————————

The secrets of the kingdom of Heaven. Jesus told His disciples they could know what the ancient sages longed to know—and He revealed those secrets in parables. In *Cracking the Code,* Lawson shows you how you can know them, too. Order #40042.

———————————

The secret of church growth. Introducing *Church Growth* and *Church Growth: Everybody's Business,* by Lawson and Tetsunano Yamamori, contain practical principles to help churches of any size to grow. Order #40002 and #40035.

Available at your Christian bookstore or

STANDARD® PUBLISHING